LUNCH
SACK
LEADERSHIP

SIMPLIFYING LOVE AND RESPECT IN LIFE AND THE WORKPLACE

K. ROB TEEL

LEGACY BOOK PUBLISHING
YourLegacyBook.com

Lunch Sack Leadership

AUTHOR: Kenneth "Rob" Teel

ILLUSTRATOR: Monkey Hub Studios, Inc.

ISBN-13: 979-8988795209

DEDICATION

To My Personal Leadership Hall of Fame

This book is dedicated to the
following leaders who had
direct authority over me
who exemplify what it
means to grow and
develop others.

Greg Pfister,
School Principle, Pastor

Delayno Robinson,
Coach, Pastor

Curt Barr,
MSgt. (USAF) (Ret)

Greg Metty,
MSgt. (USAF) (Ret)

Robert Holder,
Lt Col. (USAF) (Ret)

Duane Grlicky,
SMSgt (USAF) (Ret)

Robert Pelley,
Colonel, (USAF) (Ret)

Gerald Reeves,
CMSgt, (USAF) (Ret)

Chris Gries,
Colonel (USAF) (Ret)

Jerry Moore,
Chief Transformation Officer.
Deputy Director, OMES

Rob McClure,
Pastor

Harry M. Wyatt,
Lt General. (USAF) (Ret)

Jason Davis,
Colonel, USAF

Nathan Schlaud,
PMP, RPC Inc

Shawn Rosemarin,
VP R&D Engineering,
Pure Storage

Mrs Chesnutt,
5th Grade Teacher

Bradford Phillips,
USAF.

Greg Slavonic,
Rear Admiral (USN) (Ret)

Jim McNabb,
Pastor (Ret)

Jim Denley,
Chaplian, Colonel, (USN) (Ret)

Scott McChrystal,
Chaplain, Colonel U.S.Army (Ret)

In the grand theater of my life's journey is an illustrious Hall of Fame (seen above), a pantheon reserved for those whose guidance I was obliged to embrace. Yet, this acknowledgment would only be complete with paying homage to the myriad of leaders who, as peers and from across various organizations, have left an indelible mark on my life. To those with whom I've had the privilege of working side by side, your identities are etched in my memory. Your influence has been nothing short of transformative. Furthermore, I sincerely thank my family members and lifelong friends. You are the unsung heroes of my narrative, the constant sources of love, support, and encouragement.

TABLE OF CONTENTS

FOREWORD

In a world teeming with leadership guides and management theories, "Lunch Sack Leadership" emerges as a refreshing, innovative exploration of what it truly means to lead in the modern era. This book, penned by an astute observer of human nature and organizational dynamics, is an invitation to reimagine leadership not as a one-size-fits-all template but as a bespoke craft tailored to the unique needs and strengths of each team and situation.

This book's heart is the conviction that self-awareness is the cornerstone of effective leadership. This differs from traditional leadership models, which often emphasize control and uniformity. Instead, "Lunch Sack Leadership" proposes a more nuanced approach, recognizing that the essence of leadership lies in the ability to understand oneself and one's impact on others.

The metaphor of the lunch sack is both humble and profound. Just as every lunch sack can contain a variety of foods catering to individual tastes, effective leadership is about providing what is needed for each situation and individual. This approach challenges the outdated notion that there is a universal key to leading effectively, advocating for a more adaptable, personalized style instead.

In chapters like "Efficiency vs Authenticity" and "Common Goals, Different Styles," the author delves into the nuances of communication and team dynamics. The insight that there is no such thing as an efficient relationship underscores a fundamental truth: authentic connections, not streamlined processes, are the bedrock of successful leadership.

"Crunchy or Smooth Peanut Butter" and "Your Habits Matter" delve into the practicalities of leading diverse teams. These sections underscore the importance of understanding individual differences and the power of habit in shaping effective leadership practices.

Finally, the "Inversion-Launch Organizational Model" offers a revolutionary framework for understanding how organizations can thrive through inverted hierarchies and a focus on launching individual strengths rather than conforming to a rigid structure.

"Lunch Sack Leadership" is more than a book; it's a movement towards a more personalized, empathetic, and practical approach to leadership. As you turn these pages, prepare to challenge your preconceptions, embrace diversity, and redefine what it means to lead. Welcome to a journey that promises to transform how you lead and view the world around you.

S. Randall Allsbury

INTRODUCTION

Lunch Sack Leadership is the culmination of decades of experiences as a follower and leader. My first formal interest in leadership was born almost 30 years ago when a military supervisor handed me a copy of the book "The Seven Habits of Highly Effective People," by Dr. Stephen Covey. This work greatly influenced my life because it formalized some of what I already understood and experienced about human relationships, leadership in organized sports, student government, and the U.S. military. It also made me a life-long learner and practitioner of the Covey principles. Sometimes, I refer to Dr. Covey as "Papa Covey," intended to be a term of respect and endearment. Over the years, I have consumed dozens of works on leadership, many of which I refer to in this book. I understand reading a book does not make one an expert, but fortunately for the reader, the works and theories I reference here have all been practiced in my school of hard knocks. They have all been field-tested!

The idea of Lunch Sack Leadership began when I hosted a technology panel on culture and leadership with a group of Chief Information and Technology Officers. I walked them through the exercise and asked how they made a peanut butter and jelly sandwich. The positive response I received from the participants was overwhelming. At first, I thought this might be a one-off response, so I tried it several more times with other leaders and executives, and the positive feedback was the same. As a former business analyst and project manager, the technical complexity around the building of the sandwich resonated with me because I knew it could be used in organizational and business theory. The simplicity of using the metaphor of a peanut butter and jelly sandwich, an American household food item, disarms and encourages people to open up about their preferences, which easily translates into meaningful discussion on workplace behaviors and business systems.

I have worked in the science, technology, engineering, and mathematics (STEM) fields all my career and have had the pleasure of working alongside and being inspired by some extraordinarily intelligent people. Nothing fills the room like the egos and university degrees of intellectuals who work in the STEM fields. Another purpose of using the peanut butter and jelly sandwich as a metaphor is deconstructing the ego.

This book guides how to become a Lunch Sack Leader and transform yourself and your organization. You'll find the 6 points of hospitality contrasted with the 5 "old school" leadership attributes and the 7 points of toxic leadership. There are also the 5 points of Dynamic followership, which are accompanied by identifying different types of followers and methods on how you might lead them.

Utilizing the inversion-launch approach relies on seven fundamental concepts that ought to be applied for crafting, reorganizing, or augmenting a company or organization. Employing preference-based leadership in conjunction with the inversion-launch methodology will drive your organization, yourself, and your team to exceptional heights.

Lastly, achievement is gauged not solely by financial gains but also by the strength of our connections and the well-being of our spirit, which bestows significance and fulfillment to our existence.

Leaders stand at the intersection of transformation for positive or negative outcomes. The business decisions they make and how they interact with others will impact people emotionally, physically, financially, and spiritually. What kind of leader will you be?

CHAPTER 1

Self-Awareness: One of the Keys to Great Leadership.

In a cozy kitchen, Alex craved a classic peanut butter and jelly sandwich. Under the warm sunlight shining through the kitchen window, Alex gathered Jiff peanut butter, Welch's grape jelly, and a new loaf of Wonder bread from the cabinet.

He reached into the bread bag and, skipping the heal and first four slices, dragged two perfect pieces and placed them on a clean plate. Alex unscrewed the lid of the peanut butter jar. Alex carefully spread a generous layer of peanut butter on one slice of bread using a butter knife. The peanut butter was smooth and spread easily, satisfyingly clinging to the bread.

Then, opening the jar of grape jelly, Alex could smell the sweet aroma. Alex spread a jelly layer on the second slice of bread using a different knife to avoid mixing the flavors prematurely. The jelly glistened in the sunlight, its texture contrasting beautifully with the creamy peanut butter on the other piece of bread.

Alex enjoyed the contrasting textures and aromas. Carefully, Alex combined the slices, cut the sandwich diagonally, and admired the perfect layers of peanut butter and jelly at the edge.

Taking a bite, Alex relished the rich and sweet flavors, finding comfort in this simple delight. In that moment, the sandwich brought a sense of contentment and connection to life's simple pleasures. Alex discovered joy in the simplicity of this treat.

The idea of Lunch Sack Leadership is based upon understanding the personal preferences of self and others. Self-awareness is a journey and not a destination, but, in some instances, it is, in fact, a destination. This is true when it comes to food preferences. Most of the time, when a person tastes something they do not like, they become instantly self-aware of that fact, and it is remembered by the brain both consciously and subconsciously. Taste, smell, and sight are some of humans' most powerful senses. This is why some people don't like the texture of certain foods; while the food may taste fine to them, the texture is not right, so they prefer not to eat it. The sense of smell is similar. Take Blu-cheese, for example. It has a musty smell that could be described as dirty socks, which is too overpowering for many. They prefer not to eat it, while others don't like the smell but love the taste and sprinkle it on their salads or melt it on their burgers. Sight is also an important part of experiencing great food, which is why one of the most common phrases heard is, "Wow, that looks really good." Cabbage soup, steamed broccoli, and other cruciferous veggies might taste amazing to many. Still, the smell of boiling cabbage or steaming broccoli in the kitchen will sour the nose of many. The triple play is when you can capture smell, taste, and sight. The sizzling fajitas passing through a restaurant in a cast iron skillet is an excellent example of this. You hear the sizzling before you smell it or see it, and then turn your head, and your nose is filled with the smell of the food, and your eyes take a snapshot of that classic presentation. One might say the same as meats and vegetables from the barbeque or smoker. The possibilities and combinations of how food engages our senses are almost endless, especially when one considers all the wonderful ethnic foods around the world. **Please message me your favorite experience of food and the senses.**

LET'S CHAT

Food preferences can also be a journey depending on what's happening in a person's life. If a person has the stomach flu or is sick and not feeling well, certain foods are automatically checked off the list while others are added. There are some that, due to health or religious reasons, have restricted diets and only eat certain foods even though they may have a much broader pallet. It also depends on how certain foods are prepared, which makes a huge difference in taste and texture. A person may say they don't like steak because their family always cooked it well-done. Later in life, someone lets them try a bite of filet-mignon or prime-rib cooked medium to medium rare and vua-la. They learn they love the taste and order one cooked that way the next time they visit a steak house or fine restaurant.

Uhh... I think I'll pass... Thanks...

Another good example is whether a person mixes food on their plate. For some, the individual food items should never be touched, while others enjoy mixing certain items to create their collage of flavors.

One of the most amazing things about food is how it can trigger powerful memories. Certain experiences with the senses can sear the moment into our brains forever. I had the distinct pleasure of growing up and being raised around Mexican and Puerto Rican families, and so I was blessed at a very young age with the flavors of Latin food right off the stove of Abuela's kitchen. The smell of carnitas on the pan or barbeque still makes me homesick. Occasionally, my lunch sack would be filled with Tacos, Tamales, Taquitos, and Mofongo left over from the night before, which was much better than the normal brown bag fare, and yes…I refused to trade. "There is no way I'm giving you this tamale for a bag of barbeque chips." As a child of the 80s, there were no ethnic food aisles in the chain grocery stores, so if you wanted to try it, you had to know someone or go out to a restaurant or a specialized store. I will never forget my first experience with homemade Asian food that was not from a restaurant. I had a Korean friend in elementary school who invited me to his apartment to spend the day. At dinner time, I watched with great curiosity as his mom grabbed a wicker basket and went out to their small patio where she had a herb garden where she had planted and grown herbs and spices unavailable in the local grocery stores. After hand-picking what she needed from the garden, she started to cook, and the smell from the apartment kitchen of what I now know to be beef bulgogi was incredible, and I will never forget that first bite. My senses had been awakened as if they had been asleep. I had tasted the homemade flavors of Latin America, but this was the first time I had tasted the fresh flavors of Asia. I don't remember much about that day with my Korean friend at 12 years of age, but I will never forget his mother's cooking.

Later in college, I was involved with the African American Student Union and made some very good friends who invited me over to their parents' homes for dinner during the holidays. One of the typical desserts around the table at our house was apple and pumpkin pie. When I tasted my first piece of my friend's mother's sweet potato pie, it was so tasty, and it has remained a fond memory for many years. A similar experience happened to me again when I attended the United States Air Force Technical School at Keesler Air Force Base in Biloxi, Mississippi, where a Cajun Airman from Louisiana told me how excited he was to have a weekend pass because he was going back home to eat at his grandmother's house in Southern Louisiana. In his thick Cajun accent, he started to rattle off a bunch of dishes and foods I had never heard of. When I told him I had never tried Cajun food, his eyes lit up, and he told me he would bring me back a plate. I've been eating Cajun food ever since. I share all of this to demonstrate the power of the senses. My early years helped set the stage and preferences for a lifetime love of food from around the world and the people who prepare it. Leaders can get so caught up in being efficient in their respective business systems that they lack the capacity to connect with others more deeply and truly impact or transform culture.

Becoming self-aware is one of the most critical steps a leader can take. It creates a physiological environment that raises awareness of how one perceives and interacts with others. Looking at ourselves and understanding our personal preferences naturally makes us curious and aware of the preferences of others around us. An exercise in self-awareness for leaders is to take the time to document how they make a peanut butter and Jelly Sandwich or one of their close relatives. This is the core concept of the title for Lunch Sack Leadership because making a PBJ is surprisingly complex and varies considerably based on personal preference. Let's explore the ingredients as we discuss the topic in more detail in future chapters.

The Anatomy of the Peanut Butter & Jelly Sandwich

1. **The Bread** - "It remains one of the most widely consumed foods in the world, with at least more than 100 different types of bread available from around the globe – some of which predate many modern societies. Most bread can be categorized into sub-types, such as quick breads, flatbread, and yeast bread."[1]

2. **The Peanut Butter or Nut Butters** - "The shelves of grocery stores are dominated by three varieties of peanut butter, namely - natural or organic, creamy or smooth and chunky or crunchy. Common Nut Butters include Almond, Pistachio, Cashew, Coconut, Brazil Nut and Cashew butter.[2]

3. **The Jam or Jelly** – "Taste of Home has identified 57 different types of Jelly, Jams, and fruity spreads.[3] Author Linda J. Amendt has published a book entitled "175 Best Jams, Jellies, Marmalades & Other Soft Spreads."[4]

4. **The utensils** – the tools of the kitchen to create the masterpiece

How you approach this task may tell you a lot about your preferences and, indirectly, about your leadership style. The real value comes from when you learn how those who report to you both, directly and indirectly, prefer to be led. The sandwich is a metaphor for how you interact with them on a daily basis, and it is a guide for how you would make adjustments to optimize individual performance. Most importantly, it gives you the opportunity to care about them, which makes you a better human authentically.

CALL TO ACTION: Document how you make the sandwich by filling out the form online at: www.lunchsackleadership.com

CHAPTER 2

The One-Size-Fits-All Approach to Leadership and How it No Longer Fits

There are many examples of the One-size-fits-all approach to leadership. Let us explore some of the most common ones and their pitfalls.

a) The big conference call or Live broadcast format

One popular method for leaders to articulate their vision to a large organization is to hold big video conference calls where everyone connects and watches the leader give a speech. Most of the time, this is a monologue, which can be slightly enhanced by including a questions and answers segment in the chat where people can ask questions with their names displayed or remain anonymous. Depending on the organization's size, there will typically be a moderator or gatekeeper who fields questions to the leader. The questions served up to the leader are all easy, and any difficult questions are answered politically and not addressed. If someone has the courage not to be anonymous and puts themselves out there by asking a hard question, the poor soul may end up having a manager or director swoop in for the body slam.

The irony is almost comical after a leader insists they have an open-door policy and tells you about culture and transparency and how you can talk to them directly. All the people managers wince when a leader says this because all it takes is one individual to send a poorly worded email or ask a difficult question, and the negative ripple effect can be severe.   What usually happens is that everything is scripted, and people start scrambling when something goes off-script.   Everyone involved and listening in on the conference knows that it is scripted, which causes people to instinctively tune out.   In the end, word gets out about retribution to the person who asked the tricky question, and it chills culture.

There are some exceptions, such as when a leader holds an "ask me anything" type call with little to no gatekeeping.   It can be a useful way for a large organization to get to know a leader personally when everyone feels free to ask the same type of questions that one would ask over lunch or dinner.   Questions such as "What's your favorite sports team and why?" or What do you like to do in your free time?" "What is your daily routine?" "Do you play any sports or video games?"   This method can be especially effective if there is an opportunity for people to get to know managers, supervisors, and leaders in other departments.   In a healthy organization with good leaders, everyone should already know this kind of information about their leadership, but this is not so easy across departments.

Sharing personal information has a two-part impact on leadership.   First, it forces them to open up, be sincere, and connect meaningfully with the people they lead.   When a leader truly connects with people, the impact on culture is transformational. Second, in large organizations, it humanizes the masses who run the risk of becoming depersonalized "headcount."   Many leaders will shy away from these meaningful connections because they see it the same way a Cattle Rancher might in naming their cows.   It makes it more challenging to take Betsy and Matilda to the stockyards when they can be nameless headcount; livestock sold at a price per pound for a reduction in force.   This may touch a nerve for many leaders who think they must make "tough" personnel and "performance" decisions as part of their job description. This topic is discussed much more succinctly in Simon Sinek's book entitled "Leaders Eat Last."[5] The book opens with information about the United States Marine Corps and a story about a United States Air Force A-10 Warthog pilot flying a mission in Afghanistan. The account of this mission and the remaining contents of the book will help the leader redefine what it means to be "tough" and measure "performance."

b) Email blasts for more than 10-20 people

Emails...The bane of our existence. Long gone are the days when email communications were only for IT departments. Professionals and students in any field must work with more and more emails daily. When someone is working through hundreds of emails per day, it seems that those who chose a blue-collar trade are the smart ones. How many emails do carpenters, electricians, and truck drivers answer a day? One might argue that they don't make as much money as the computer screen worshipers but think again.

An ancient saying is, "The sleep of a laborer is sweet, whether they eat little or much, but as for the rich, their abundance (and too many emails) permits them no sleep."[6]

The point here is not that we should be Luddites but that there is a line to be drawn in the sand somewhere with the number of emails sent and received daily. A good barometer is a task-based message to 10 people or the project teams a person works with directly. A quick scroll through anyone's inbox will reveal dozens, if not hundreds, of emails with mostly unusable information. The advent of instant messaging via Microsoft Teams or Slack has helped some because it allows people to include emojis and gifs to convey tone more effectively and be more direct and conversational. Email blasts to large groups trying to convey a personal, cultural, or emotional message are rarely effective. Some informational email blasts can be quite useful, for example, a message saying the office is closed for the holiday or who won the chili cookoff. Some of this is personal preference, and the key to good email communication is knowing your teams' cumulative personal tastes. "A new culture-building approach is already in place at some organizations, one in which everyone is responsible. Importantly, this model doesn't relegate culture-building to an amorphous concept that everyone influences, but no one leads or is accountable for. Shared responsibility for culture throughout an organization involves different people and functions within the organization playing different roles in developing and maintaining the culture."[7]

If a Lean Six-Sigma trained professional were to analyze how to be more efficient at emails, they would end up being ninth-degree black belts. Their first initiative is to remove the reply-all button. Some of these email strings are like watching the same 25-car pile-up video repeatedly. Whether you start from the top of a message and work down or scroll to the bottom and work up, it can be mind-numbing, especially when there is finger-pointing. Somewhere around the 3rd reply, it becomes clear that using typed words to communicate is almost entirely useless. It occurs to no one that they can pick up the phone and call, start a virtual meeting, or even better, go to the person's office or bring the team into a conference room for an in-person work session. If these kinds of emails are what you deal with most of the day, it's no wonder you're stressed out. One recommendation is to take a ten-minute break and watch RC Plane crash compilation videos. There is a mysterious connection between the time wasted on emails and watching beautiful RC planes with thousands of hours and dollars poured into them crash to the earth. A close second might be Domino Fails. Though not quite as expensive as an RC plane, the time to set up the dominos is probably equal. It's all about preferences, so if watching crashing RC planes and Domino Fails is not your idea of a mental break, then pick your poison. **Please message me with your go-to 10-minute stress reliever.**

LET'S CHAT

If you must use emails, make them transactional yet personal and for sharing information. However, file sharing and tools such as Adobe Sign, DocuSign and BlueInk have replaced document sharing and workflows. The idea is that your emails should be personal, fun, and concise. If fun is not allowed at your office or is not your personal preference, then gratitude helps and will help you and others around you relax and smile more. Email is not a document management system, enterprise resource planning system (ERP), customer relationship management system (CRM) or an IT Service Management System (ITSM) or any other Line of Business Application. Any attempts to use it for these purposes create chaos.

It is also a tool that limits mass communication, building personal relationships, leading, creating, influencing, and sustaining company culture.

c) Meeting formats

There are a few different ways to conduct meetings, much like emails, which can be the bane of one's existence when not done properly. The formal meeting might consist of an agenda and a presentation. If the meeting concerns a project, it may focus on deliverables, timelines, resources, and stakeholders. A technical meeting may include work sessions for a team to collaborate, troubleshoot, and problem-solve. There are also one-on-one and large meetings, both virtually and in person. Depending on the source, there are up to 15-20 meetings with various creative formats sandwiched in between.[8] Elise Keith, the Co-Founder of Lucid the Meeting Innovation Company and author of *Where the Action Is: The Meetings That Make or Break Your Organization*, has some precious insights with valuable diagrams. She has a compelling argument that every meeting has a human connection outcome and a work outcome, along with other theories that corroborate and are complimentary to the concept of Lunch Sack Leadership.

There are three main types of meetings, each serving different purposes and involving distinct groups of individuals:

a. Informal team meetings, where a familiar group of individuals who know each other well come together regularly.

b. Structured gatherings, like kickoffs, ideation sessions, and workshops, convened to address specific requirements.

c. Meetings involving two separate groups with a noticeable "them-and-us" dynamic, coming together in response to an event, such as interviews, broadcast meetings, and negotiations.[9]

d. The key, according to Keith and the Lucid team, is that we must know the leadership styles of participants and that "outside of regular team meetings, some should be explicitly designed to establish positive relationships.[10]

How would you change how you communicate and meet with others if you knew the positive or negative impact your methods had on morale?

CALL TO ACTION: Sign into your email account and analyze the quantity and quality with the intent of replacing a percentage of emails with actual conversations.

CHAPTER 3

Efficiency vs Authenticity – "There is No Such Thing as an Efficient Relationship" (Covey)

The challenges of work and life can have a cumulative wear-and-tear effect on human's capacity to be authentic. Sinicism erodes morale like water erodes the side of a mountain, and our emotional survival instincts create facades to protect our true heart. Like a digital avatar, many will create multiple personas where there is a professional and personal version of themselves. Some business cultures try to mold you into their image, and any straying from that orthodox version of a "professional" can negatively impact your promotion or advancement. Being authentic is not always easy and should not be confused with sharing everything with everyone because having boundaries is important. Your co-workers may not be people you would confide in, and that's ok because you have the autonomy to limit how much you want to tell others about yourself. What's important is that your interaction with people is a sincere representation of the real you. Pretending you like someone or are interested in them only to get ahead, complete a project, or meet a revenue or performance goal is where the trouble is. This is often referred to as manipulation. Manipulation is one of the key ingredients needed to create a Molotov cocktail for toxic organizational culture. The key is to honor the limits you set for yourself so that your interactions with others are always genuine. There is a difference between being courteous and doing your best to get along with others to encourage teamwork and being deliberately manipulative. Beware when motive and intent are not pure and untrustworthy. Winning hearts and minds with a compelling intellectual argument or use case is different than emotionally manipulating others behind the scenes or publicly.

Many leaders fall into the trap of efficiency over authenticity and always seem to need more reasonable justification for their less-than-excellent approach to professional relationships. In his book The Seven Habits of Highly Effective People, Stephen Covey describes these types of interactions with others as transactional relationships vs. transformational ones.[11] He also spends some time discussing how relationships are viewed personally and professionally. Much of our global economy is built around what he describes as a win-lose model, like a game of chess or checkers: I win, you lose, or I lose, and you win. The same goes for arguments in relationships where one person feels like they have to prove they're right and the other person is wrong, which generally ends up with someone having their feelings hurt or angry.

There are times when there is a clear right or wrong answer to things like in mathematics, but more often when it comes to winning and losing, it is a matter of preference. Is there a wrong way to make a peanut butter and jelly sandwich? Possibly because everyone thinks the way they make the sandwich is far superior to all others, especially those whose worldview is wrongly wrapped around winning and losing at all things in life.

How would the winner be determined if two people or teams were provided with all the ingredients to make the sandwich? You could set a timer to see who could make one the fastest, but quality would likely be compromised. The people or teams would not take the time to make it the way they like it and would end up with a sandwich they did not care for, which would not be a win for them but a loss. Sure, they made the sandwich quickly and won on paper, but it was a loss in the end for them because the quantities of peanut butter or jelly weren't quite right. Another method would be to have each team measure the ingredients perfectly and then cut the bread of each sandwich with a certain level of precision. Each person or team would be able to take as much time as needed to create and present "the perfect" sandwich that will be measured in millimeters and weight, and then winners and losers will be declared. The point here is that it is possible to create a win-win scenario with almost everything in life, which means that a leader can assign someone to make a PBJ in business and life, and it can be done precisely how they like it. This means the entity assigning you the task is 100% pleased with the results, and you are 100% happy with the results, which is a win-win. One might even say that anything in the 95 percentile is a win, but that is for each entity and individual to decide mutually. It is not always easy to achieve the win-win results and there can be layers of complexity when solving for personal or business challenges. Still, with courage, consideration, and a little extra effort everyone can get there.

"Many people think in either/or terms in business and personal relationships. They think if you're nice, you're not tough. But Win/Win is nice ... and tough. It's twice as tough as Win/Lose. To go for Win/Win, you not only have to be nice, you have to be courageous. You not only have to be empathic, you have to be confident. You not only have to be considerate and sensitive, you have to be brave. To do that, to achieve that balance between courage and consideration, is the essence of real maturity and is fundamental to Win/Win."[12] People will go into a negotiation or meeting very confidently but without being intentionally considerate of the others in the room, and it will likely end in a win-lose. They will have the courage of convictions but won't be considerate of others. They will compensate for their lack of internal maturity and emotional strength by borrowing strength from their position, power, or credentials.[13]   For example, someone might have impressive credentials such as a PhD in Legumes (nut studies) or an advanced engineering degree in Pomology (fruit studies). While it is valuable to have subject matter experts in the room, it is very important for both the short and long term to do the hard work of a win-win. The focus should be on the issues, not on personalities or positions. If corners are cut, it will lower trust, performance, and happiness over time. Interestingly, there is a solid argument to be made that not everyone's opinion holds the same value. It does not mean that people are not intrinsically valuable but that their ideas and competencies are not all on an equal playing field.   Ray Dalio advocates for a meritocracy where people's opinions and ideas are weighted based on several factors. He had a creative way of measuring team members using a baseball card stats method.[14] The win-win concept is built on the foundation that everyone at the table shares a certain level of competency in their respective areas. For example, if there is a Medical Doctors conference on podiatry, one would expect the people presenting at the conference to be leading podiatrists, not ear, nose, and throat Doctors. Although meritocracy, as described by Dalio and many others, is valuable, Lunch Sack Leadership focuses on making minor meaningful adjustments to accommodate the preferences of others who share a similar goal. The peanut butter and jelly sandwich is a metaphor for this. Ed Deming argued for similar leadership adjustments in his famous 14 key principles. He was the author of Quality Productivity and Competitive Position, Out of the Crisis (1982–1986), and The New Economics for Industry, Government, Education (1993), and books on statistics and sampling. While all his 14 key principles are valuable, let's focus on the two most relevant to win-lose, lose-win, win-win and people's preferences.

First, "Break down barriers and competition between departments. People in research, design, sales, and production must work as a team to foresee problems of production and usage that may be encountered with the product or service." Second, eliminate slogans, exhortations, and targets for the workforce, asking for zero defects and new levels of productivity. Such exhortations only create adversarial relationships, as the bulk of the causes of low quality and low productivity belong to the system and thus lie beyond the power of the workforce."[15] Keep in mind that the failures of these "systems," that Deming is referring to are invariably created by leadership. Instead of taking responsibility for a failed design, leaders blame the workers for not executing their own bad ideas properly.

In summary, Deming advocates eliminating internal competition and reducing statistical variation by improving the quality of systems.   In manufacturing and other business systems, these improvements may only be fractions of a percentage plus or minus, but they make a difference.   These axioms hold true with how leaders interact with and inspire people by being aware of and honoring the personal preferences of others.

There is a group of individuals whose entire worldview in their business and personal life is built around competition between winners and losers, and they need help internalizing the concept of win-win or something mutually beneficial and rewarding. Winning at almost any cost is at the core of their character. "Although they might verbally express happiness for others' success, inwardly, they are eating their hearts out. Their sense of worth comes from being compared, and someone else's success, to some degree, means their failure. Only so many people can be Vice President; only one person can be "number one." To "win" means to "beat."[16] It's the second place is the first loser crowd. Their sandwich must always be the best or at least in the top 5 of all PBJs ever made, the GOAT in the PBJ Hall of Fame. While this attitude might work in sports, it falls short in many of the most important areas of life. One of the key pillars of Lunch Sack leadership is shared with the words of Papa Covey: "Victory does not mean victory over other people. It means success in effective interaction that brings mutually beneficial results to everyone involved. It means working together, communicating together, making things happen together that even the same people couldn't make happen by working independently."[17] This only comes from a person with character that is whole and full of integrity and authenticity.

Leaders will argue that they must be efficient and don't have the time to authentically interact with and engage with others and their personal preferences. One-on-one meetings with these types of leaders are like taking a car through an automatic car wash; everyone gets the same treatment. The left tire is locked into the motorized track. They put the car in neutral and take their hands off the steering wheel, and then someone pushes the big red button to roll through. A platitude of encouragement is sprayed here and there, and then "tough feedback" is given at the end when the loud dryer turns on, and you get the green light to drive away. The leader pretends to be authentic by asking a few personal questions. Still, the lack of sincerity shines through, and people are left with the sinking feeling that the rare annual or semi-annual interaction with leadership was checking a box. They could care less about how you like your PBJ, and it's doubtful they have any idea that you have a peanut allergy. They will keep serving you the same sandwich made the way that they think everyone should consume it. Some leaders truly care about those around them but are unsure or unwilling to adjust to accommodate others. Modern technology has made the excuses about it taking too much time obsolete. Name an eating establishment or coffee shop where a person cannot customize an order. Each establishment likely sees hundreds of customers per day with various preferences and dietary restrictions that they gladly accommodate. Making small preference-based adjustments on how a leader interacts with peers and followers is transformative. These seemingly small adjustments are precisely the quality level that Deming refers to in several of his key principles and can change a business task into a valuable and authentic interpersonal interaction. The authenticity discussed here is focused on humility and should not be confused with collectivism or consensus. It is not about everyone getting together to vote someone off the island like the "reality" TV show Survivor, which is a perversion of what it means to lead and be a member of a team. It should also not be confused with being soft because sometimes it is necessary to terminate a toxic team member who is undermining the team by being rude, hostile, manipulative, or a bully. This type of hospitality of honoring preferences is encapsulated in 8,000 years of sacred writings from the Sumerians, Judaism, Greek Philosophy, Christianity, Islam, Buddhism, and Hinduism. What makes an interaction with a leader sacred? Remember when you received authentic positive feedback from a respected leader, parent, or friend or when valuable advice was given? If you can remember it, and it made a lasting impact on you and others, then that moment in time becomes sacred. Leaders must take the time to understand you, to truly care, and to be courteous. To be authentic.

CALL TO ACTION:

Take a few minutes and reflect on the times you received meaningful positive feedback from someone you respected or loved. **Write them down and refer to them as a compass when you lead and interact with others.**

LET'S CHAT

CHAPTER 4

Common Goals Different Styles – The Art of Fighting without Fighting

"What's Your Style?"

Enter the Dragon is a classic 1973 martial arts film directed by Robert Clouse, written by Michael Allin, and starring Bruce Lee.[18] Lee is a highly proficient martial arts instructor from Hong Kong and is approached by a British intelligence agent named Braithwaite, who is investigating a suspected crime lord named Han. Lee is persuaded to attend and participate in a high-profile martial arts tournament on Han's private island to gather evidence proving Han's involvement in organized crime. The only way to the island is by boat, and Bruce Lee and several tournament participants board a ship for the journey. One of the participants, named Parsons, decides to pass the time at sea by bullying some sailors. As he makes his way around to Bruce Lee, he taunts and asks him, "What's your style?" Lee replies, "You could call it the art of fighting without fighting." Parsons asks Bruce Lee to "show him some of it." Lee insists that there is not enough room on the boat to demonstrate his style and convinces the bully to get on a dinghy to a smaller nearby island. Once Parsons is on the boat, Lee hands the rope to the sailors the bully had been pushing around, and they laugh and watch the boat sink along with Parsons. This was Bruce Lee's art of fighting without fighting.

I recommend watching it; a quick internet search will pull up the classic video clip.

LET'S CHAT

There are dozens of personality assessments available for those interested in becoming more self-aware and understanding how they interact with others interpersonally and in teams. I have taken the 5 Voices, DISC, Meyers-Briggs, The Flag Page, and the 4 Lenses and facilitated courses on several assessments. After being exposed to the methodology and science of all these, it is a fun activity to try and identify the personality types of movie characters. Keep in mind that some scriptwriters are much more proficient and gifted at developing characters than others, so depending on the movie and the quality of the acting, it may range in ease and difficulty.

One thing that is certain in all areas of personal and professional life is that you will experience conflict with others, especially when it comes to problem-solving. Even many math problems seemingly free of personality and emotion have more than one way to solve. If there is more than one way to solve a math problem, rest assured, there will be multiple ways to solve problems in life and business. Your way is likely one of many ways. The rugged and rigid leadership arguments for hard facts, science, and numbers soften, which is again what Deming argues in his key principles, such as eliminating quotas. Of course, numbers and science are critical, but how they are used for problem-solving and profit-making is another matter altogether. Intentionally choosing work and life methods that make you and/or your team happy and fulfilled is possible and preferred. Everyone gets the sandwich how they like it. These methods are found in the world's most successful companies and the happiest families and relationships. Ideally, this does not mean compromise. It creates a win-win.

Simon Sinek touches on the happiness of a positive workplace and the toxicity of a negative one in his book Leader's Eat Last, where he discusses the effects on human physiology and how it impacts hormone levels such as cortisol, dopamine, and oxytocin.[19] Many have heard of the popular Tuckman's theory about the five stages of team development. It was first proposed by psychologist Bruce Tuckman in 1965. It stated that teams would go through 5 stages of development: forming, storming, norming, performing, and adjourning.[20] These stages supposedly start when the group first meets and last until the project ends.

One of the most important things you can do as an individual contributor or team member is to become self-aware. The maturity of individuals and teams can be measured by how quickly they move through the five stages of team development. With mathematics, the whole is equal to the sum of its parts, which is why some teams get stuck in the storming and norming phases and never achieve high-performance levels. This again is peering through the eyes of Deming, where he deemphasizes basing performance on numbers alone. There is something dynamic about a team. Every team sport has a position that individual players hold, and their role is to execute specific tasks in that position. All team sports have offensive and defensive components. We often hear commentators and coaches say, " They're one of the best centers or forwards in the game." What makes them the best? Is it their numbers alone? Another common saying is that a player may have great field or court vision. How exactly is that measured? I was recently watching the Wimbledon match where IBM, alongside the Hawk-Eye Line calling system, seemed to have digitally mapped the entire court to about the size of a dime. This line-calling system uses multiple camera angles to trace the tennis ball's trajectory. Hawk-Eye uses six or more computer-linked television cameras situated around the court. The computer processes the video in real time and tracks the path of the tennis ball on each camera. These six separate views are then combined to produce an accurate 3D representation of the ball's path. This is extraordinarily cool and impressive technology, but it falls short of determining the intangible idea of court vision. Similarly, the numbers record certain offensive and defensive plays, while others are less of an exact science. For example, a basketball player may record a blocked shot or a defensive rebound, but how is it measured if they have good defensive posture and prevent shots? How is it measured when a player is in position relative to a successful offensive or defensive play? Sports analogies abound, but it's clear that teams are dynamic by nature and that each player relies on the skills of the others to achieve a winning result. This cooperation is what creates the exciting moments that people buy tickets to watch or pay to stream. Teams that move from norming to performing are wholes that are greater than the sum of their parts because together, they create something intangible without diminishing the individual contributions and preferences of the team members. An excellent example of teamwork is in American Football when the kicker, normally the smallest player in size, tackles a punt returner with a certain level of defensive fervor. I encourage you to take a moment and search for "best kicker tackles." This is usually the job of physically larger special teams, but if the player returning the ball gets past all that special team's defense, the last man to beat is the kicker, and there is nothing more gratifying than watching a kicker lay down an excellent tackle to prevent a touchdown.

Musical performances are another good example of team dynamics when played by multiple instruments. No matter the musical genre you enjoy, the amount of teamwork it takes to create and play great music is undeniable, and it is dynamic in nature because of the unique art that the band, orchestra, or producers create. This is why someone can recognize when a cover band is playing their favorite song vs. the original artist. It is also why an orchestra might play every note on the page with technical precision but without the virtuosity and emotion intended by the composer.

Who are you, what position do you play, what is your style? In chapter one, we used food preferences to discuss self-awareness, and now, in chapter four, martial arts and team sports, there is more science to personalities than what someone likes to eat for breakfast, lunch, and dinner. Various types of assessment are available to help people understand themselves mentally, physically, spiritually, and emotionally.

Big Five Inventory-2 (BFI-2) is the latest version of a tool for assessing the Big Five personality traits, which it labels as Extroversion, Agreeableness, Conscientiousness, Negative Emotionality, and Open-Mindedness, as well as facets of each. It is employed in psychological research and can be used for personal assessment.[21]

The Revised NEO Personality Inventory (NEO PI-R) is a revised version of a tool originally named after the Big Five trait factors of Neuroticism, Extroversion, and Openness to Experience. However, the current tool also assesses Agreeableness and Conscientiousness, plus 30 more specific traits within each factor. It is used in psychological research.

The HEXACO Personality Inventory-Revised (HEXACO-PI-R) is used to measure six dimensions of personality based on the HEXACO model. They include factors that correspond to the Big Five, as well as the factor of Honesty–Humility. It is employed in psychological research and can be used for personal assessment.[22]

The Hogan Personality Inventory (HPI) is based on the five-factor model and intended for predicting work performance, including in job candidates. Its scales are organized based on work-relevant characteristics such as ambition, sociability, and interpersonal sensitivity.[23]

The Myers Briggs Type Indicator (MBTI) assigns individuals a psychological "type" summarized in four of eight possible letters: Extroversion (E) or Introversion (I); Sensing (S) or Intuiting (N); Thinking (T) or Feeling (F); and Judging (J) or Perceiving (P). The results combine into one of 16 types, such as ENTJ or ISFP. The MBTI is widely used in business—such as for employee evaluation or during seminars—and unofficial versions are available for personal use. However, scientists often cite its limitations, including that its separate "types" oversimplify personality differences.[24]

DISC or DiSC is the name given to a collection of personality assessments that assign individuals one of four types or a blend of the types: Dominance (D), Influence (I), Steadiness (S), and Conscientiousness (C). Like the Myers-Briggs, it is promoted for use in learning about individual differences within organizations but is generally not favored by contemporary personality scientists.[25]

The Five Voices is based on the science that people don't know their leadership voice or how to use it. Some don't know what it is, others are insecure in their voice and have been told it is unimportant, and others immaturely overuse their voice and dominate the airwaves. The 5 Voices is designed to help individuals discover their leadership voice and be empowered to use it effectively.[26]

Some of the most brilliant minds will blow off these types of assessments as soft-skills nonsense. Big dominant personalities or hyper-intellectual engineers and scientists are the stereotypical culprits. The strongest desire for them is to be the most intelligent and competent person in the room. One of their favorite sayings is, "Facts don't care about people's feelings." They confuse being courteous and authentic as weaknesses, and they regularly look for opportunities to elevate themselves by proving others are wrong, always being the first to correct a person for less than 100% accurate information, 98% is not close enough. Their higher level of intelligence has helped them achieve rank and title, and many leaders, out of fear of losing the individual's intellectual property, will custom design organizations or departments around their personalities even when they are toxic. Sadly, "the unspoken standard in American sports, business, medicine, and academia is: *"The more often you are right and the more often you win, the bigger jerk you can be."*[27] Toxic behavior should not be tolerated no matter how tolerated and smart you are. In most places, being a toxic bully is seen as a character flaw—but is tolerated when people are more talented, smarter, more difficult to replace, and endowed with a higher natural success rate than ordinary mortals. "Extraordinary talent" is an all-purpose justification for tolerating, pampering, and kissing up to these destructive jerks. Our societal standard appears to be: *"If you are a really big winner, you can get away with being a really big jacka**."*[28] Angela Duckworth has some outstanding research that dispels the talent always wins belief by articulating that "someone twice as talented but half as hardworking as another person might reach the same level of skill but still produce dramatically less over time. Without effort, talent is nothing more than your unmet potential."[29] This begs the question for leaders by asking how much effort they're putting into treating their employees well. "Well" is the operative word here and means much more than just competitive compensation. This was Ray Dalio's argument that because he was paying people so well, they should give him a pass on his toxic behavior, much like an indulgence that Martin Luther condemned in his 95 Theses in 1517. Yes, the nasty idea has been around for a long time. In the Middle Ages, the sale of indulgences by the church became a controversial practice, with some critics arguing that it encouraged people to buy their way out of sin and avoid true repentance. The people who could afford the indulgences were comparatively rich.

Interestingly, many of these intellectuals are unique because they could lean towards Asperger's Syndrome and have difficulty relating to others in team and social environments. Also, among the leadership ranks, one will find a fair number of people who have attention deficit disorder (ADD). This should garner a certain level of empathy from those who must follow these types of leaders. The good news is people with Asperger's or ADD accelerate at life in dozens of areas because of their ability to focus keenly is simply unmatched. The important thing is that they're self-aware, live with this knowledge, and recognize how their behaviors might impact others. Like many things in life, those needing these assessments the most are also their biggest detractors. One can be confident that if work interaction is toxic and insensitive, so are the personal relationships with partners, friends, children, and extended family. The fact is that everyone should take a personality assessment.

Enter the Dragon; when the bully Parsons starts pushing the sailors around, the immediate reaction for many is a desire to respond with anger and self-defense. To win and beat the bully using physical force. Although the scene ends with a win-lose scenario where Lee wins and the bully loses, it is done without Lee throwing a single blow. The maturity and wisdom of Lee's response is both transformational and transcendent. That's the power of becoming self-aware and knowing your style; it allows you to operate optimally and observe how others do the same within the context of a team. You've taken the time to assess exactly how you like your peanut butter and jelly sandwich, and now, because you've done the hard work of documenting all that information, it is easier for you to see how others prefer to make theirs. This helps you be a better person and team member.

Previously, we discussed toxic leaders and how many organizations and departments are designed around catering to them to retain the "smartest" people. This is a good example of an organization engaging in the wrong team design. The leaders that scoff at personality assessments and soft skills are still making personality-based design decisions for all the wrong reasons. They enable the worst kinds of behaviors and rotate out good people who refuse to be treated poorly by the monster they've created in a co-dependent corporate culture.

The platitudes and cynicism are plentiful, such as "You haven't missed a paycheck, have you?" "We've hit our numbers the last three quarters. I don't see what the problem is?" "Didn't you just receive a big annual bonus?" "Have you seen our customer rating? It's the best it's been in a year." **Message me the best excuses you've heard for lousy behavior and culture.**

LET'S CHAT

The opposite of all this toxicity is to be intentional about culture and team design and to build and work in high-performing, happy teams. There is merit to the argument that culture must be created organically and may vary with each team and department; there is a lot of science around the subject of organizational behavior in academia and business. Suppose you're a leader and have an opportunity to build a team from scratch or reshape a current team. In that case, I highly recommend diving in to learn more about being intentional with organizational behavior. Something you can do immediately is to learn more about yourself and those you're currently working with. If you take an assessment and learn your strengths and weaknesses, then focus on your strengths and hire for your weaknesses. On the surface, this looks like a selfish move, but the key is that the team should ultimately be built around the mission, not you. Decisions on building a high-performing team should be based on bringing the best people together to accomplish the goal or mission, and the only way to know who's the best suited is to be aware of yourself and others. To know your style and the style and preferences of others.

Some will take an assessment and be paralyzed by what they perceive as weakness vs strength. They will expel tremendous mental, emotional, and spiritual energy trying to "fix or improve" their weaknesses. This creates a high jacking of the mind, soul, and spirit. STOP! Of course, people always have room to improve, but this should be viewed on a continuum, not in a lose-win pity party. It takes a self-aware and mature person to understand how they truly thrive. If someone takes an assessment and all they see is weakness, comparison, and inferiority, then a spiritual problem can only be repaired and made whole by spiritual means. Let me assure you there is hope and healing for you. Please see the appendix for recommended readings.

CALL TO ACTION: Take a personality assessment of your choice. If you have taken one recently, refer to it. If it's been more than three years, take a refresher.

CHAPTER 5

Why the Long Tail in the Bell Curve Works in Teams – The Long Tail

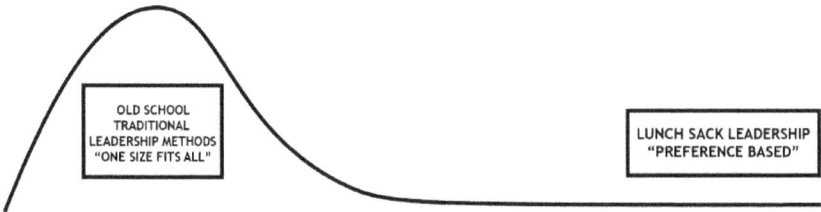

The boutique model works because it's what people are used to now.

"The Long Tail" by Chris Anderson is a book that explores the concept of the "long tail" and how it applies to the world of business and commerce.[30] The long tail refers to the vast and often overlooked market of niche products and services beyond the most popular items. Anderson argues that with the rise of the Information Age, the long tail has become more accessible to consumers and businesses alike. Companies like Amazon and Netflix have been able to tap into this market by offering a wide selection of products and services that cater to specific interests and preferences. The book explains how the long tail can be leveraged by businesses to increase their profits and grow their customer base. It also explores the cultural and economic implications of the long tail, such as the democratization of production and the shift from mass culture to niche culture. Customized products found on Etsy and Redbubble are also good examples of this. This is a massive cultural shift away from brick and mortar and large "blue-chip" retailers such as Walmart, Target, Best Buy, Home Depot, Lowes, Macy's, and Kohls to name a few. Certainly, these retailers still have plenty to offer, but previously, substantial wealth was required to purchase a custom-made item.

A Wharton business school paper challenges the economics of the long-tail theory, specifically around demand concentration, product variety, and the power of popular brands.[31] Still, it does not dispute the cultural shift around people's buying habits. This goes beyond digitizing physical products on the shelves for online purchase; it is about being able to customize based on preference. The popular shoe company Vans and others have sites where you can design your own shoe almost from scratch with dozens of color and style combinations. Let's take Pam, for example. She is a new employee of a local manufacturing company and has two sons, Johnny and Billy, ages 10 and 12. Johnny just received a $100 gift card for his birthday from Vans and went online and custom ordered himself a pair of shoes exactly how he wanted them, and they arrived in 5 business days. Though Pam is a single mother and needs an adjusted work schedule to drop her kids off and pick them up from school daily, she is only given two shift options, which are incredibly challenging for her to meet under the public school schedule. The company providing her with only two shift options is, in essence, saying, "We're very excited to have a person of your talent and skill be a part of our team, but you only have two types of shoes to pick from." Pam begrudgingly accepts this, but in the back of her mind, she is asking why. Hundreds of retail companies are providing the same service as Vans. Yet, most work environments and their leadership still operate under the old brick-and-mortar retail model where a customer's choices are limited to what the store has in stock. It's a much bigger issue than just accommodating employees' schedules. Many leaders take this assembly-line approach with their teams and direct reports, applying a one-size-fits-all method that is disingenuous and uninspiring.

A leader might argue that they do have flexible work schedules, which is certainly a part of meeting people's needs and preferences, but Lunch Sack Leadership goes much deeper than this. If a massive section of the market is going to a custom niche model for the lifestyle preferences of everyone who reports to you, why aren't you? In chapter one, we asked that you take the time to document exactly how you make a PBJ, and you were likely surprised at the level of detail and all the steps. What would prevent you from doing the same with the preferences of your employees and teams?

One of the primary challenges to the Lunch Sack Leadership methodology is that the other non-preference-based leadership methods and styles have worked for the last 50 years and achieved some amazing results and business success. There are plenty of stories of business profits accomplished with traditional methods. For example, former CEO of General Electric, Jack Welch, grew the company substantially, and his methods included the controversial "rank and yank" employee termination system — contrasting Welch's popular American methodology with that of the Japanese during the same era. In Japan, it was a cultural norm for chief executives to take personal responsibility for any failures or adverse events under their leadership, including layoffs. This cultural expectation is known as "responsibility to society" or "social responsibility," and it was deeply ingrained in Japanese business culture. When a Japanese company had to lay off employees, it was not uncommon for the CEO to resign to take responsibility for the decision. This was seen as a way of upholding the company's social responsibility and maintaining trust with stakeholders, including employees, customers, and shareholders.

This practice is rooted in Japan's Confucian traditions, emphasizing social harmony and responsibility. In Japan, business leaders are expected to prioritize the needs of their employees and society as a whole rather than just focusing on short-term profits. While this practice has been criticized for creating a culture of scapegoating, it also reflects a deep sense of corporate responsibility and commitment to social welfare. It starkly contrasts the practices of many Western companies, where CEOs often receive large bonuses and severance packages even when they preside over mass layoffs or other adverse events.

You may be perfectly satisfied with your current results, so why change? Detroit auto-manufacturers were satisfied with their results but were dominated by Japan for 40 + years because Japan used Demings's methods and his 14 key principles, primal among them is reducing statistical variation. "The Japanese were also greatly influenced by another American management expert, Joseph M. Juran, who visited Japan in 1954. In a Harvard Business Review article, Juran says that Japan would have achieved world-quality leadership without his and Deming's advice, but "we did provide them a jump start, without which ... the job might have taken longer, but they would still be ahead of the United States in the quality revolution."[32]

If you're already getting results in the 88-93 percentile, is it worth the effort to close the gap and adjust to try something new? Deming believed most American managers are too stubborn to make the necessary changes. "Who do you think will be ahead five years from now?" he asked at a 1991 meeting on the Hill. "Knowledge crosses borders without visas, and there is no substitute for knowledge."[33]

The global economy and technology have broken down many barriers to communication, and it has impacted company culture. Several things differentiate leadership styles and business cultures. Since we've referred to the Americans Deming and Juran, who spent most of their careers in Japan, let's look at a few of the differences between two broad groups: American and Asian.

Communication Style: Asian business culture emphasizes indirect communication, while American business culture values direct communication. In Asian cultures, nonverbal cues and subtle language are often used to convey meaning, while Americans tend to speak more directly and use clear language.

Hierarchy: In many Asian cultures, there is a strong emphasis on hierarchy and respect for seniority. In contrast, American businesses tend to be less hierarchical, with more emphasis on individual achievement and less on formal titles and positions.

Decision-making process: In Asian cultures, decisions are often made through a group consensus process that involves input from various stakeholders. In contrast, American businesses tend to make decisions more hierarchical and top-down.

Relationship building: In many Asian cultures, building strong personal relationships is seen as essential for successful business relationships. While relationships are still important in the US, business is often more transactional.

These cultural differences can affect business conduct, including communication, decision-making, and work practices. Understanding and respecting these differences can be essential for successful business relationships. I have worked on projects where the team consisted of people from Japan, India, the Netherlands, South Africa, America, Singapore, and Brazil, all on the same active project or video conference. If you were a team leader with such ethnic diversity, you must intentionally understand culture and preferences.

Common Luxury Uncommon Hospitality

For millennia, luxury was only attainable by the very wealthy. The rarer the item or luxury service, the more valuable and henceforth the creation of all the sayings and idioms known today, such as "dinner fit for a king, lap of luxury, living large or to live like a prince, queen, or princess." A custom-tailored suit, dress pair of dress shoes or heels, or anything custom was out of reach price-wise and unattainable unless traveling to New York, London, Chicago, France, or Italy. Many of these services are available and accessible to everyone, and people's buying habits have significantly changed and lean towards sophisticated personal preferences. Of course, what is considered luxury is subjective and is usually decided by outside societal and cultural influences.

Luxury can be defined as something that is considered to be rare, expensive, and exclusive. It is often associated with high-quality, prestigious, and indulgent experiences, products, and services that are beyond the reach of most people. It can take many forms and vary widely depending on culture, social status, and personal preferences. Some common examples of luxury goods and services include designer clothing and accessories, high-end cars, private jets, luxury hotels and resorts, fine dining experiences, and expensive jewelry and watches. Luxury is generally associated with the highest levels of quality, craftsmanship, and attention to detail. Products and services considered luxurious often come with a premium price tag and are designed to provide an elevated experience that is only available to some.

In addition to physical products and experiences, luxury can also be associated with intangible qualities such as exclusivity, prestige, and status. For example, owning a rare and highly sought-after item can be considered a luxury because it sets the owner apart from others and elevates their status in the eyes of their peers. What is considered luxury can vary widely depending on individual tastes and preferences. Still, it is generally associated with high-quality, exclusive, and indulgent experiences, products, and services that are beyond the reach of most people.

Personalized experiences that are designed to provide the utmost comfort, convenience, and indulgence to individuals who are willing to pay a premium price for them. Luxury services are often associated with the world's most affluent individuals, who demand the best quality and highest service. They are often customized to meet each client's specific needs and preferences and are delivered with the utmost professionalism and discretion. The price tag for luxury services can be very high, reflecting the premium quality and exclusivity of the experience. The definition and price of luxury and customized services have evolved with the information age because of the increased accessibility, which Anderson articulates in the Long-Tail. The customized Vans ordered by Johnny did not break the bank.

Several global brands specialize in the commercial hospitality industry. They provide exceptional service and care to guests, exceeding the standard expectations. It is about creating a personalized and unique experience for guests that leaves a lasting impression and builds a deep connection between the guest and the establishment.

This level of hospitality is often associated with luxury hotels and resorts, but it can also be found in smaller boutique hotels, bed and breakfasts, and vacation rentals. It is characterized by attention to detail, anticipation of guest needs, and a willingness to go above and beyond to exceed expectations. Some examples of hospitality include a personalized welcome where guests are greeted by name upon arrival, and the hotel staff takes the time to learn about their preferences and interests to tailor their stay accordingly. There is attention to detail in every aspect of the guest experience, which is carefully considered, from the linens' quality to the room's amenities selection. Customized experiences are created where the staff works with guests to create unique and memorable experiences tailored to their interests, such as private tours of local attractions or exclusive dining experiences. Seamless service is provided as staff anticipates guest needs and is always available to provide assistance, ensuring a stress-free experience.

The business establishment providing the hospitality demonstrates genuine care and warmth towards guests, making them feel welcome and valued throughout their stay. Hospitality is about delivering a high level of service and creating a memorable and emotional connection with guests. It is about making guests feel at home, even far away from home, and providing them with an experience they will never forget. It would be easy to argue that this is what people are paying for, but this level of hospitality is rare.

So, what makes hospitality so uncommon in the workplace? Showing hospitality to a friend, family member, or co-worker is an act of kindness and generosity that can help strengthen relationships and create a sense of culture and community. It is the "Long Tail." It involves creating a welcoming and comfortable environment that makes the other person feel valued and appreciated.

As a leader, let's imagine your next one-on-one meeting with a direct report or peer in the following format:

1. **Welcome them warmly:** Greet the person with a warm smile and a friendly hug or handshake. Let them know that you are happy to see them and that they are welcome in your workplace.

1. Welcome Them Warmly

2. **Offer refreshments:** Offer the person something to drink or eat, such as coffee, tea, or a light snack. Ask them if they have any dietary restrictions or preferences.

2. Offer Refreshments

3. **Provide a comfortable space:** Make sure the person has a comfortable place to sit and relax. Offer them a comfortable chair or couch.

3. Provide A Comfortable Space

4. **Engage in conversation:** Engage the person in conversation and ask them about their day, interests, and thoughts. Try using humor and laughing with them. Show genuine interest in what they say and be a good listener. This cannot be faked and must be sincere, or it will be seen and perceived as manipulation.

4. Engage In Conversation

5. **Show appreciation:** Express your gratitude to the person and your relationship.

5. Show Appreciation

Let them know you value their friendship or work relationship and are grateful for their presence. Discuss any challenges respectfully.

6. **Offer Assistance:** If the person needs help with anything, offer your assistance. Whether it's helping them with a task or providing guidance and support, let them know that you are there to help. This is only accomplished through good listening and communication.

6. Offer Assistance

Overall, showing hospitality as a leader is about creating a warm and welcoming environment that makes the other

person feel comfortable and appreciated, even though that might include challenging performance feedback. Being honest with them is an act of kindness that can help strengthen trust in relationships and create a sense of community. If you followed the suggestions above, you created a unique and meaningful "luxury" experience for someone, costing you no more than a cup of coffee or tea. For them, it was free but invaluable. You gave them the PBJ exactly how they preferred it. **What's the best example of hospitality shown to you by a leader?**

This can be contrasted with the "old school" Jack Welch system of interacting with employees, also known as "rank and yank" or "forced ranking," which was a controversial system implemented by the former General Electric CEO in the 1980s and 1990s. The method involved evaluating employees annually and ranking them from best to worst performers. The bottom 10% of employees were then targeted for termination, regardless of their actual performance. Similarly, a "postmortem documentary on Enron called The Smartest Guys in the Room. During the company's ascendancy, it developed a performance review system for Enron that graded employees annually and summarily fired the bottom 15%. In other words, no matter what your absolute level of performance, if you were weak relative to others, you got fired."[34]

Proponents of the system argued that it incentivized high performance and weeded out underperforming employees, leading to a more competitive and productive workforce. However, critics argued that the system created a toxic work environment and encouraged employee cutthroat competition. They also pointed out that the system was often based on subjective evaluations and did not consider external factors affecting employee performance. For example, someone may have had a health issue, and a major family event occurred within a calendar or fiscal year, so their performance suffered. This is not to argue that ranking performance is not valuable, but it must be accompanied by a robust performance management and coaching system. Many performance management systems that could be more robust are unscientific or incomplete.

Despite its controversies, many companies widely adopted the "rank and yank" system in the 1990s and early 2000s, and it persists because it's seared into the minds of many leaders as an effective way to achieve success. Interestingly, it was also used as a primary method to reduce headcount at Enron. However, in recent years, many organizations have moved away from this approach, recognizing its negative impact on employee morale and retention. Today, many companies are instead focusing on continuous performance management, where feedback and coaching are provided on an ongoing basis to help employees improve their performance and reach their full potential.

As a leader, let's imagine a different type of one-on-one meeting with a direct report or peer in the legacy format with the following "old school" attributes:

1. **Lack of empathy:** Leaders need more empathy towards their employees or customers.

1. Lack Of Empathy

They may be unable to understand or relate to the challenges others face and may not consider their concerns or needs when making decisions. "Just get it done!"

2. **Self-centeredness:** The leader may be focused solely on their interests and priorities without considering the impact of their actions on others. They may be willing to sacrifice the well-being of others for their own personal gain or success. "You're making me look bad!"

3. **Poor communication:** The leader may need to communicate better with their employees or customers, leading to misunderstandings and confusion. They may not take the time to listen to others' concerns or feedback and may dismiss their ideas or suggestions without considering their value. "This is not what I was looking for!"

4. **Lack of respect:** The leader may need more respect for their employees or customers, treating them as expendable resources rather than valuable contributors to the business's success. They may need to take the time to acknowledge others' hard work or contributions and may not provide opportunities for growth and development. "If you and your team can't do this, others in line would be happy to!"

4. Lack Of Respect

5. **Lack of integrity:** The leader may need more integrity and make dishonest or unethical decisions. They may prioritize their interests over the well-being of others and may engage in behaviors that harm others or the business as a whole. "I'm asking you not-so-nicely to go create the 5% that we missed on our quota so we can hit our numbers this quarter." **What's the most disingenuous and inconsiderate feedback you've received?**

5. Lack Of Integrity

An inconsiderate and uncaring business leader can create a negative work environment affecting morale, productivity, and success. A business leader with Uncommon Hospitality demonstrates empathy, respect, and integrity toward others to build strong relationships, foster a positive work culture, and drive success.

Psychological safety at work refers to employees feeling comfortable taking interpersonal risks, such as speaking up, making suggestions, and admitting mistakes, without fear of negative consequences to their job security, status, or self-worth.

When employees feel psychologically safe at work, they are more likely to share their opinions, ask for feedback, collaborate with colleagues, and take on challenging tasks. They are also more likely to be creative, innovative, and committed to their work, as they feel valued and respected by their colleagues and supervisors.

On the other hand, when employees do not feel psychologically safe, they may become disengaged, anxious, or defensive. They may avoid speaking up, withholding information, or engaging in unproductive behaviors, such as blaming others or avoiding responsibility. This can result in lower productivity, reduced creativity, and decreased job satisfaction for the individual employee and the team.

Several factors contribute to psychological safety at work. One of the most important is leadership. Managers and supervisors who model open communication, active listening, and empathy create an environment where employees feel heard and supported. They also set expectations for respectful and constructive interactions among team members.

Other factors contributing to psychological safety include clear expectations and goals, feedback and recognition, trust among team members, and a culture of continuous learning and improvement. It is essential for organizations to create policies and practices that support these factors and to regularly evaluate their effectiveness in promoting psychological safety.

Psychological safety is a critical component of a healthy and productive workplace. Organizations can encourage creativity, collaboration, and innovation by fostering an environment where employees feel comfortable taking interpersonal risks. This can lead to improved performance, increased job satisfaction, and better overall outcomes for both employees and the organization.

Robert I. Sutton explores the harmful effects of workplace bullying and toxic behavior. His works are extraordinarily well-researched and full of quantifiable examples. The story of Bob Sutton's colleague, "Mr. X," who was a brilliant engineer and notorious jerk. Despite his impressive technical skills, Mr. X's abusive behavior drove away talented employees and created a toxic work environment. Mr. X's behavior towards Sutton was described as rude, dismissive, and condescending. Mr. X was known for regularly mistreating his colleagues and subordinates, and his behavior created a horrible work environment that negatively affected the entire organization.[35] So, what is toxic leadership? We have touched on it briefly in other chapters. Toxic leadership is a behavior that is harmful, abusive, or destructive to individuals, teams, and organizations.

Here are some examples of toxic leadership:

- **Micromanagement:** When a leader excessively controls and monitors their team's work to the point where it stifles creativity and innovation. (Not to be confused with Management by Inspection Active and Passive)

1. Micromanagement

- **Bullying and Intimidation:** Leaders who use fear, threats, or belittling to control or manipulate their team.

2. Bullying & Intimidation

- **Lack of Transparency:** Leaders who withhold information, keep secrets, or make decisions behind closed doors can create a culture of distrust and suspicion.

- **Unfair Treatment:** Leaders who show favoritism, discriminate against specific individuals or groups, or make decisions based on personal biases.

- **Lack of Accountability:** Leaders who do not take responsibility for their actions or mistakes or blame others for their failures.

- **Toxic Communication:** Leaders who use aggressive or passive-aggressive communication styles or engage in gossip or rumor-spreading can create a culture of negativity and division.

- **Arrogance and Ego:** Leaders who have an inflated sense of self-importance, put their own needs above those of the team, or take credit for others' successes.

7. Arrogance And Ego

These are just a few examples of toxic leadership behaviors that can harm individuals and teams, damage morale and productivity, and ultimately harm the organization. **Give some examples of toxic leadership you have experienced.**

LET'S CHAT

CALL TO ACTION:

1. Think of a simple adjustment you can make in your personal and business relationships that would show hospitality.
2. Identify toxic behaviors that are currently demonstrated by you and your organization and eliminate them.

CHAPTER 6

Crunchy Peanut Butter or Smooth

Customizing programs alongside personal and team habits creates gritty and strong employees and teams, not weak ones. Nice and crunchy! What are the ingredients that make up a resilient individual and team? These are the people who show up every day physically present and intellectually engaged. Not only do they bring a high level of intellect to the table, but they're also enthusiastic, contribute creative ideas, and show a prowess for thinking outside the box. Previously, we discussed how certain personality types are more inclined to some of these attributes than others, such as introverts and extroverts. Still, there are common competencies that separate high-performing teams and individuals from the pack.

The book "Grit" by Angela Duckworth explores this concept. It defines grit as a combination of passion and perseverance and discusses how it contributes to success in various domains, including education, sports, and business. One of the primary sources for her research was the United States Military Academies. The acceptance requirements are some of the most selective in the world. To be accepted to a United States Military Academy, applicants must have a high school diploma or equivalent with a high grade-point average (3.8-4.0) and meet specific academic requirements, including high minimum scores on standardized tests like the SAT or ACT. Generally, those who apply to the academy are also excellent athletes and are captains of their respective high school teams. To be accepted, they must meet specific physical fitness and medical standards. They must pass a medical exam, meet height and weight requirements, and pass a physical fitness test. Applicants must also demonstrate good character, leadership potential, and a desire to serve their country and be nominated by a U.S. Senator, Representative, Vice President, or the President. The admissions process is highly competitive, and acceptance is based on a holistic review of academic, physical, and personal qualifications. While each of the five service academies (West Point, Naval Academy, Air Force Academy, Coast Guard Academy, and Merchant Marine Academy) has its own specific requirements and application process, the high standards required for admission assemble an elite and talented freshmen class year over year that is in the top 10% of the nation. Students who are used to being the best at everything in life are now "racked and stacked" against peers who are as good or better than they are in every category, which can challenge them to the core because they suddenly find themselves standing amongst a thousand Valedictorians, star quarterbacks, and team captains. This creates a unique dynamic that makes certain students rise to the top 1-2% of the 10%.

Through research and real-life examples, Duckworth shows that talent alone is not enough for success; the willingness to work hard and persist through challenges leads to achievement. She also provides insights on developing grit, including cultivating a growth mindset, finding purpose, and developing habits of discipline and deliberate practice. The combination of passion and perseverance is a crucial factor in achieving success. While talent and intelligence are important, they must be more on their own because effort and practice matter more than natural ability.

People willing to work hard and persist through challenges are more likely to achieve their goals than those who rely solely on talent. The good news for those who might think they're less gritty than others is that Duckworth suggests grit can be developed and cultivated over time. She offers insights and practical advice on developing grit, including cultivating a growth mindset, finding purpose, and developing habits of discipline and deliberate practice. She shows that grit is valuable for the military and important in various domains, including education, sports, and business, and she provides examples of individuals who have demonstrated grit and achieved success in these areas.

The importance of perseverance in overcoming obstacles and setbacks is highly emphasized, and she shows that those who persist through challenges are more likely to achieve their goals than those who give up easily.

Developing and maintaining a growth mindset is one of the keys to effective leadership. Becoming self-aware and understanding and accommodating the preferences of others will help them become top performers and you a better leader. This is what separates true leadership from executive title holders. Jeremie Kubisek uses the analogy of the Nepalese Sherpa, who helps teams summit Mount Everest. "The successful Sherpas never keep track of how many times they have summited Mount Everest, but they know exactly how many people they have helped make the summit."[36] Leadership is not about you – it's about using your developed skills and talents to impact and influence others around you in a positive way to help them reach their potential.

The poor and toxic leadership we often observe results from someone developing very bad habits over time and not adopting a growth mindset. Here's the bad news: most toxic leaders are unaware of their negative behaviors and lack the will to identify their shortcomings or character defects and make a change. Some tests and assessments can help identify toxic leadership used in military and business environments. Toxic leadership can hurt unit morale, mission effectiveness, overall readiness, productivity, and organizational performance. Therefore, it is important to identify and address toxic leadership behavior as early as possible.

Multi-Source Assessment and Feedback (MSAF): MSAF is a 360-degree assessment tool that allows subordinates, peers, and superiors to provide feedback on a leader's performance, including their leadership style, interpersonal skills, and communication ability.[37]

Command Climate Survey (CCS): The CCS is a survey designed to assess a unit's overall morale and climate. It can provide valuable feedback on the level of trust, respect, and communication within the unit and help identify potential issues related to toxic leadership.[38]

Behavioral Event Interview (BEI): The BEI is a structured interview that assesses a leader's behavior in specific situations. It can help identify leadership strengths and weaknesses and potential issues related to toxic leadership.[39]

Leader 360 Assessment: This survey collects feedback from various sources to comprehensively evaluate a leader's behavior, decision-making, and effectiveness.[40]

Organizational Culture Assessment Instrument (OCAI): This assessment measures an organization's culture along six dimensions, including its values, beliefs, and practices. It can help identify areas where toxic leadership behavior may contribute to a negative organizational culture.[41]

Emotional Intelligence (EQ) Assessment: This assessment measures an individual's ability to recognize, understand, and manage their own emotions and the emotions of others. It can help identify leaders exhibiting toxic behavior due to a lack of emotional intelligence.[42]

Leadership Effectiveness Analysis (LEA): This assessment measures a leader's effectiveness based on a range of factors, including their ability to inspire others, communicate effectively, and manage conflict. It can help identify leaders who may be exhibiting toxic behavior that impacts their effectiveness.[43]

These assessments can help identify potential issues related to toxic leadership and can inform strategies for addressing these issues through leadership development, counseling, and other interventions. It is important to note, however, that these assessments could be more foolproof and should be used in conjunction with other leadership development and training efforts. Remember Demings' model on reducing statistical variation through quality improvement? Please make no mistake: it takes courage to become self-aware and be willing to take some of these assessments and be evaluated by your peers and direct reports. I know the word "intervention" may cause some to squirm, but it is not uncommon. Ray Dalio, the founder of Bridgewater Associates and author of the book "Principles: Life and Work,"[44] describes a personal intervention led by his colleagues at Bridgewater, who were concerned about his leadership style and its impact on the company culture. His colleagues felt that he was too domineering and abrasive in his interactions with others and that his style was causing fear and tension within the organization. The intervention involved several of his colleagues sharing their honest feedback about his behavior, and he acknowledged their concerns and committed to changing his leadership style. Dalio writes that the intervention was a turning point for him and that it led him to develop the principles-based approach to leadership and decision-making that he now advocates for. He emphasizes the importance of radical transparency and radical honesty in creating a culture of openness and accountability, and he attributes his transformation as a leader to the feedback he received during the intervention. Dalio's personal intervention is a powerful example of the importance of self-awareness and openness to feedback in personal and professional growth, and it underscores the value of creating a culture of transparency and honesty in organizations.

So, how does one develop good habits that stick and overcome bad and often toxic ones? "Atomic Habits"[45] by James Clear argues that the key to lasting behavior change lies in small, incremental improvements that compound over time. He introduces the concept of "atomic habits," which are small, consistent actions that are easy to do but add up to significant results. He emphasizes that the focus should not be on achieving specific goals but rather on developing a system of habits that supports a desired outcome. The concepts are divided into four parts, each addressing a different aspect of habit formation. Part one focuses on the importance of making small changes that lead to significant results. Part two explains how to create good habits by making them obvious, attractive, easy, and satisfying. Part three discusses breaking bad habits by making them invisible, unattractive, complicated, and unsatisfying. Part four explains how to make habits stick by incorporating them into one's identity and creating a supportive environment. Clear draws on research from various fields, including psychology, neuroscience, and sociology, to explain why habits form and how they can be changed. He also includes numerous real-world examples and practical exercises to help readers apply the concepts to their own lives. None of this is easy, but most things in life that are worth fighting for are difficult.

Get some grit, change your bad habits, and adopt good ones. The science is in; all your excuses for not changing and becoming a better leader are now like the old saying about your lowest human orifice. *"Excuses are like ……....; everybody has one."*

KEY POINT: Leading teams and individuals based on their preferences does not make leaders weak or less effective.

CALL TO ACTION:

1. Identify several habits you would like to start or change.
2. How might the preference-based leadership style make your team more gritty?

CHAPTER 7

Leadership & Teamwork

The ultimate example of teamwork can be found in competitive sports. A quick scan of all the events in the Olympics would provide a good baseline. Pick a sport that involves more than one person to win, and the analogies are almost endless. The same holds true for solo musicians vs playing in an orchestra. The good news for Olympic athletes and competitors is that whether they're part of the curling or Jamaican bobsled team, at the end of every match, each player gets to go home alive, even when they lose. There is another higher level of teamwork forged in the furnace of danger; enter the world of the military and first responders, where stakes are much higher than taking home a trophy or a gold medal. While everyone is inspired by the stories of great teams on ESPN and sports television, no one is more qualified to talk about teamwork than a first responder or military veteran. The victors are not carried off the field, court, or ice on someone's shoulders; there is no standing ovation; their reward is going home to their loved ones with a heartbeat, knowing they helped save the lives of others. This is a different kind of leader altogether because it represents the Holy Trinity of excellence in human behavior: leadership, followership, and teamwork.

The study of leadership and the development of leadership theories can be traced back to the early 20th century. One of the earliest leadership theories is the "Great Man Theory," which suggests that great leaders are born with inherent traits that make them natural leaders. This theory emerged in the 19th century but gained prominence in the early 20th century.

Around the same time, the Trait Theory of leadership emerged, focusing on identifying traits that influential leaders possess. Researchers attempted to identify a set of traits that were believed to be characteristic of successful leaders.

As the years progressed, various other leadership theories were developed, including the Behavioral Theories that shifted the focus from innate traits to observable behaviors of leaders. The Contingency Theories, such as Fiedler's Contingency Model and Hersey-Blanchard's Situational Leadership Theory, also emerged, emphasizing the importance of situational factors in leadership effectiveness. The early to mid-20th century saw the development and documentation of some of the foundational leadership theories that laid the groundwork for the extensive research and diverse perspectives on leadership that continue to evolve today.

We will focus on three models that have been curated for consumption and combined into a usable model for Lunch Sack Leadership. The three models used and referenced are the Full Range Leadership Model, Dynamic Followership, and Meta-Leadership. Each one will be explored and reviewed in detail, including the specific terminology used by the original authors and creators of the models. The United States Air Force Squadron Officer School curriculum also analyzes these concepts in-depth. Lunch Sack Leadership combines the three models as a new and innovative measure for individual and team performance. Bernard M. Bass and Bruce J. Avolio developed the Full Range Leadership Model (FRLM). The model is a leadership theory that describes various leadership styles along a continuum, ranging from transformational leadership to transactional leadership. Bernard Bass initially introduced the transformational leadership concept, and later, in collaboration with Bruce Avolio, they expanded the model to include both transformational and transactional leadership behaviors. Ira Chaleff developed the concept of dynamic followership. In his book "The Courageous

Follower: Standing Up to and for Our Leaders," Chaleff introduced the idea of dynamic followership to emphasize the importance of followers in the leadership dynamic. He argued that effective followership involves being compliant and actively engaged, thinking critically, and contributing to the organization's success. Chaleff's work highlights the reciprocal relationship between leaders and followers, emphasizing the need for followers to be dynamic, adaptive, and willing to challenge when necessary for the overall benefit of the group or organization. There have also been some significant works by Robert E. Kelley, Robert L. Taylor, and William E. Rosenbach, in their work entitled "In Praise of Followers," in Military Leadership: In Pursuit of Excellence," where the others identify the follower types of Sheep, Yes People, Alienated Followers, and Effective Followers. The concept of meta-leadership was developed by Dr. Leonard J. Marcus, Dr. Barry C. Dorn, and Joseph M. Henderson. They introduced the idea in their book "Renegotiating Health Care: Resolving Conflict to Build Collaboration," published in 1995. The concept of meta-leadership focuses on leadership that goes beyond traditional hierarchical structures and involves individuals who can collaborate across organizational and professional boundaries to address complex challenges.

In the context of health care, where the concept was initially applied, meta-leadership involves leaders who can work collaboratively with stakeholders from various sectors to address public health issues. The concept has since been extended to other domains, emphasizing the importance of leaders who can navigate and influence networks and systems beyond their immediate organizational boundaries.

"Team of Teams" by Stanley McChrystal is a management book that explores the challenges of leading organizations in today's rapidly changing and complex world.[46] McChrystal draws on his experience as a US military general in Iraq to demonstrate how traditional hierarchical structures and decision-making processes are inadequate in the face of unpredictable and decentralized threats. McChrystal argues that organizations must adapt to this new reality by becoming more agile, collaborative, and decentralized. He introduces the concept of a "team of teams," which involves breaking down silos and creating a network of smaller, self-organizing teams that can quickly respond to changing circumstances. The book is divided into three parts. First, he describes the evolution of warfare and the challenges faced by the US military in Iraq. Second, he discusses the need for organizations to become more agile and collaborative in response to complex and unpredictable challenges. Third, he provides practical guidance on implementing the team of team's model in organizations. Throughout the book, McChrystal emphasizes the importance of clear communication, trust, and a shared sense of purpose in building effective teams. He also discusses the need for leaders to relinquish control and empower their subordinates to make decisions and take action. Before you dismiss his analysis as only applying to military scenarios, he takes the time to outline the business application of his theories carefully. He uses some examples to support his arguments.

Meta-leadership is a leadership approach that emphasizes the importance of collaboration, communication, and adaptability in addressing complex problems and crises.[47] It involves leaders at different levels and from different sectors working together to create a shared vision and coordinated response to challenges. It focuses on building trust and relationships between stakeholders, including government officials, business leaders, community organizations, and citizens. It emphasizes the importance of effective communication, understanding, and working with diverse perspectives and interests. Like Team of Teams, Meta-leadership also recognizes the need for flexibility and adaptability in responding to changing circumstances and emerging challenges. It emphasizes the importance of ongoing learning and development and the ability to quickly and effectively adapt to new information and circumstances. It is a collaborative approach emphasizing the importance of working together across boundaries and sectors to address complex challenges and achieve shared goals. This model uses a compass to illustrate the different parts of an organization, such as leading up, down, across, and beyond. In the context of meta-leadership, "up" refers to the ability to lead and influence those in positions of authority above you, such as higher-level government officials or organizational leaders. "Down" refers to the ability to lead and influence those who report to you or are lower in the organizational hierarchy. "Across" refers to collaborating and working effectively with peers and colleagues within your organization or sector.

Finally, "beyond" refers to engaging with stakeholders outside your immediate organization or sector, such as community groups, the media, or other external partners. Together, these dimensions of leadership in meta-leadership emphasize the importance of building relationships and working effectively across different levels and sectors to address complex challenges and achieve shared goals. By leveraging their influence and relationships up, down, across, and beyond, meta-leaders can mobilize resources and build coalitions to create meaningful change.

Dynamic followership is a concept that refers to the proactive and engaged role that followers can play in contributing to the success of a team, organization, or community. It involves a set of behaviors, attitudes, and skills that enable followers to work effectively with leaders and contribute to achieving shared goals.[48]

(See illustration on the next page.)

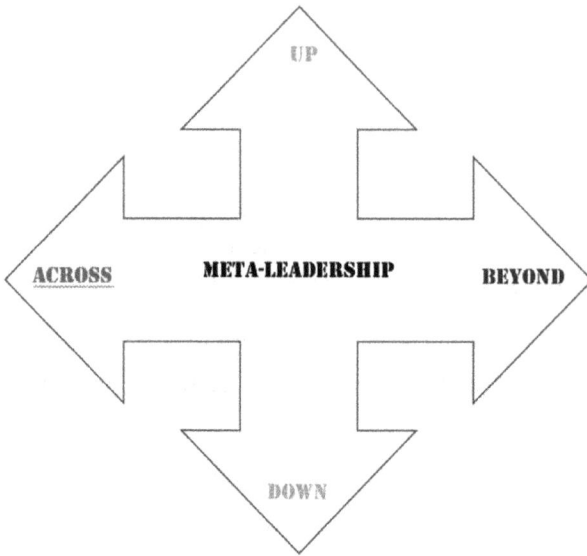

UP

ACROSS   **META-LEADERSHIP**   **BEYOND**

DOWN

There are several components of dynamic followership, including:

Self-awareness: Dynamic followers are self-aware and have a clear understanding of their strengths, weaknesses, values, and goals. They use this self-awareness to take ownership of their contributions and seek opportunities for growth and development.

1. Self Awareness

Active engagement: They are actively engaged in their work and are committed to achieving their goals. They take initiative and proactively seek opportunities to contribute to their team or organization.

Critical thinking: They can think critically and analyze complex problems or situations. They can generate creative solutions and make informed decisions that contribute to the success of their team or organization.

Effective communication: Dynamic followers can communicate effectively with others, both verbally and nonverbally.

They listen actively and ask questions to ensure they understand others' perspectives and express their ideas and feedback clearly and respectfully.

Collaboration: They can collaborate effectively with others and work well in a team environment.

They understand the importance of building relationships and trust, and they can work collaboratively to achieve shared goals.

Dynamic followership is a critical component of effective leadership and teamwork. By taking ownership of their contributions, engaging actively, thinking critically, communicating effectively, and collaborating with others, dynamic followers can make meaningful contributions to the success of their team or organization.[49]

In the dynamic followership model, there are several types of followers, including alienated followers, sheep, yes people, and effective followers:[50]

Alienated followers: These are followers who feel disconnected from their work, their team, or their organization. They may feel that their contributions should be valued or their voice should be heard. Alienated followers may need to be more engaged, cynical, and skeptical of their leaders and the organization's goals.

Alienated Followers

Stuck with the extra paperwork, AGAIN!

Maybe if someone asked for my suggestions, we wouldn't have all of this!

Like they care, anyway...

"They fulfill their roles passively because of some offense which led them to become cynical and distance themselves from leadership and gradually sink into disgruntled acquiescence."[51]

Sheep: These followers go along with whatever their leaders tell them to do without questioning or challenging their decisions. They may need more initiative and rely on their leaders for direction and guidance. Sheep may be seen as passive and unengaged.

Yes-People: These are followers eager to please their leaders and may agree with their decisions and ideas without critically evaluating them. Yes, people may need more independent thinking and may be more focused on pleasing their leaders than on achieving shared goals.

Yes People

Effective followers: These are followers who are actively engaged, think critically, and contribute to the success of their team or organization. Effective followers are self-aware, take initiative, communicate effectively, and collaborate well with others.

Effective Followers

They are able to think independently and challenge their leaders when necessary while still remaining committed to achieving shared goals. The dynamic followership model emphasizes the importance of followers who are actively engaged, think critically, and contribute to the success of their team or organization. Effective followers balance their needs and goals with those of their team or organization and work collaboratively to achieve shared goals. In contrast, alienated followers, sheep, and, yes, people may hinder the success of the team or organization by being disengaged, passive, or overly compliant with their leaders. Below is a diagram of the different types of followers.

52

The Full Range Leadership Model (FRLM) is a leadership theory that describes different leadership styles and their impact on organizational outcomes. Bernard Bass and Bruce Avolio developed it, which has been widely used in academic and organizational settings.[53]

LAISSEZ FAIRE	TRANSACTIONAL		TRANSFORMATIONAL			
Hands - Off Leadership	Management by Exception (MBE)	Contingent Reward (CR)	Individual Consideration (IC)	Intellectual Stimulation (IS)	Inspirational Motivation (IM)	Idealized Influence (II)
	Passive	Active					

54

The Full Range Leadership Model describes three main types of leadership styles: transactional, transformational, and laissez-faire. Transactional leaders use rewards and punishments to motivate followers, while transformational leaders inspire and motivate followers through vision, charisma, and personal relationships. Laissez-faire leaders provide little guidance or support to followers, allowing them to make decisions and solve problems independently. The model also includes several sub-dimensions of each style, such as contingent rewards (CR) and management-by-exception (MBE-A, MBE-P) for transactional leadership, individualized consideration (IC), inspirational motivation (IM), idealized influence (II) and intellectual stimulation (IS) for transformational leadership, and passive management-by-exception for laissez-faire leadership. Let's look at each one of these individually.

Hands – Off Leadership

You've got a brain! You can figure it out!

Transactional Leadership

Management By Exception -Active or Passive

"MBE may take two forms: active (MBE-A) or passive (MBE-P). During the active approach, leaders actively monitor followers for deviations from standards in the form of mistakes or errors and take corrective action as necessary. Utilizing an active approach may become necessary and effective in some situations, particularly when safety is a factor. During MBE-P or the passive approach, leaders passively take corrective action only when they feel they must get involved, which is usually too late. Unfortunately, when leaders supervise large numbers of followers, it may be difficult for them to monitor all members actively. However, when leaders deliberately wait until a situation is out of control before intervening, this is a passive approach."

In MBE-A, adherence to rules, regulations, and performance standards is enforced to regulate followers. This approach emphasizes meticulous observation, specific guidance, and hands-on oversight to enhance organizational effectiveness. Central to this philosophy is the idea that leaders should target nonconformity, errors, and subpar performance that stray from the norm. MBE-A implements this by actively searching for and rectifying deviations from expected behavior, aiming to address non-compliance promptly.

Again, American auto-manufacturing comes into view and is contrasted against Ed Deming's fourteen principles. MBE-A is transactional because it focuses on deviation from standards and has its place in certain critical situations, but when overused, it becomes aggressive micromanagement, which is universally disliked.

Management By Exception

Passive

It looks like you did this all in the wrong format. You'll need to go back and change it.

A passive approach to MBE is when a leader waits for a process to crash and burn before getting involved and taking action fully. The problem with this approach is that it is solely focused on negative performance and rarely on the positive accomplishments of an individual or team. This creates a culture of low trust, fear, and complacency.

Contingent Reward (CR)

Contingent reward involves a mutually beneficial interaction between leaders and followers. This constructive dynamic involves leaders outlining performance standards that must be met and utilizing rewards to reinforce positive achievements. It's seen as a potent way to motivate followers by establishing clear and consistent expectations. CR operates on an implicit agreement that delineates expectations for all involved parties. In this transaction, leaders define performance objectives, offer guidance to fulfill these expectations and provide rewards or assistance as followers attain desired results. Meeting all performance expectations becomes pivotal for followers to attain these shared goals and receive the contingent reward.

CR also offers followers guidance on how to reach their performance objectives. When leaders delineate organizational goals and values, it empowers members to achieve more significant results. Moreover, setting these shared expectations fosters higher levels of trust and commitment among followers.

Sales compensation systems are one of the first places to look when trying to find rodents and spiders in a toxic work culture with subpar performance results compared to competitors.

To be clear, I'm not referring to individuals as rodents and spiders but instead poorly designed self-destructive business systems. Ones that provide an organization with a win on paper but a long list of angry customers and unhappy employees who compete with one another for the scraps. If not careful, an ill-devised system for bonuses and commissions can create a Pavlov's Dog response from a team and get ugly. Jack Welch's "rank and yank" system exemplifies a flawed Contingent Reward model. A positive Contingent Reward is when a leader provides rewards and incentives to their followers in exchange for achieving specific goals or performance standards from a well-designed system. Leaders who practice contingent rewards establish clear performance expectations and provide their followers with specific goals. They also offer incentives and rewards, such as bonuses or promotions, to those who meet or exceed these expectations.

Additionally, they provide feedback and coaching to help their followers improve their performance. By using contingent reward as a tool, leaders can create a culture of accountability and performance within their team. They establish clear expectations and provide their followers with the resources and support they need to achieve their goals. This can lead to increased motivation and productivity, as team members are incentivized to perform at their best. Contingent Reward is just one component of leadership, and it should be used in conjunction with other attributes of transformational leadership to create a well-rounded approach.

Transformational Leadership

"In contrast with transactional leadership, transformational leadership involves creating personal relationships with followers that raise their level of motivation and morality. A transformational leader is attentive to follower's needs and preferences and strives to help them reach their fullest potential."[55]

Intellectual Stimulation (IS)

Leaders who practice intellectual stimulation inspire their followers to challenge their assumptions, beliefs, and values and to think critically about problems and situations. They encourage their team to explore new ideas, to take risks, and to experiment with different approaches.

By doing so, leaders foster an environment of innovation and creativity and empower their teams to reach their full potential. Intellectual stimulation is a crucial component of transformational leadership, as it helps to foster a culture of learning and development. Leaders who practice intellectual stimulation are unafraid to challenge the status quo and always look for new and better ways to do things. By promoting continuous learning and growth, leaders can inspire their followers to become more engaged, motivated, and productive, ultimately leading to greater success for the organization.

Individual Consideration (IC)

If leadership, followership, and teamwork are the Holy Trinity of Meta-Leadership, then Individual Consideration encapsulates the essence of and is the apex of Lunch Sack Leadership. This is a leader's ability to support and develop their followers individually, considering their unique strengths, weaknesses, needs, and aspirations. Leaders who practice individual consideration are attentive to their followers' personal and professional development and work to create a supportive and nurturing environment in which their team members can thrive. They provide their followers with personalized feedback, coaching, and mentoring, and they take the time to understand their individual goals and aspirations. Leaders who practice individual consideration build strong and trusting relationships with their team members by showing genuine concern for their followers' well-being and development.

They create a sense of belonging and loyalty within their team, increasing engagement, motivation, and job satisfaction.

This is an important component of transformational leadership, as it enables leaders to create a highly motivated and engaged team committed to achieving its goals. By supporting their followers' preferences, individual growth, and development, leaders can develop a culture of excellence and continuous improvement within the organization.

Inspirational Motivation (IM)

Inspirational Motivation is a leader's ability to inspire and motivate their followers through a compelling vision and a sense of purpose. Leaders who practice inspirational motivation can articulate a clear and compelling vision of the future, one that inspires their followers to achieve great things. They communicate this vision in a way that resonates with their team members, helping them see how their contributions fit into the larger picture. They also set high standards for performance by carefully balancing some of the components of Management by Exception, and they work to create a sense of urgency and excitement around achieving their goals.

Inspirational Motivation

By inspiring and motivating their followers in this way, leaders who practice inspirational motivation can create a sense of shared purpose and commitment within their team. They foster a culture of excellence in which team members constantly strive to improve and achieve their full potential. Inspirational motivation is essential to transformational leadership, as it helps create a highly motivated and engaged team committed to achieving its goals. They inspire their followers with a compelling vision and a sense of purpose for the greater good.

Idealized Influence (II)

Idealized influence is a leader's ability to serve as a role model and to be seen as a source of inspiration and admiration by their followers. Leaders who practice idealized influence are respected and admired by their followers, who view them as ethical, trustworthy, and honest. It is the well-known motto to "lead by example" by demonstrating the values and behaviors they expect from their team members. They can also build strong relationships with their followers, creating a sense of trust and loyalty within the team. By serving as a positive role model, leaders who practice idealized influence inspire their followers to emulate their behavior and to adopt their values. They create a culture of high ethical standards in which team members are motivated to act in the organization's and its stakeholders' best interests. It is easy to see how Inspirational Motivation and Idealized Influence complement one another. Good leaders are fluid in both these attributes and simultaneously inspire by leading by example. It is important that leaders do not turn leading by example into competition. Leading by example doesn't always mean working the longest hours or being the first to arrive in the office parking lot at 6:00 AM. It does not mean a leader is up at 2AM, still working and sending emails (unless it's an emergency or critical deadline).

Idealized Influence

Suppose a leader plans to exhibit the transformational attribute of Intellectual Stimulation. In that case, they will need some rest and sleep to reset the mind and balance the soul for sustainable daily operations. In previous chapters, we discussed an organization's win-lose and win-win perspectives. This is particularly relevant to Idealized Influence because those who are highly scripted in win-lose will try to outperform everyone around them. Sending emails at all hours of the morning and night because you're trying to "lead by example" can send the wrong message that you don't trust your team. When I first started my career in the military, I could be referred to as what is known as gung-ho or ate-up (I still proudly wear these titles, although in a different capacity). I had something to prove, so I would wake up extra early every day and be the first one at the shop on base to make coffee. My supervisor would start showing up even earlier, and it became a competition to see who would be the first one to get the shop. Since I was yet to be enlightened by the works of Papa Stephen Covey, I was still highly scripted in win-lose, so if he got to the office before me, I counted it as a loss. This led to me arriving at the office 45 minutes to an hour before the start time for the win. While some may find this behavior inspiring for young, motivated airmen, it is not always the most effective approach to Idealized Influence because, unlike sports, life is not a competition. Balance is the key, and Idealized Influence should always be checked and balanced against Individual Consideration and what's truly the best course of action for the individuals and teams you lead.

The Full Range Leadership Model suggests that transformational leadership is the most effective style, leading to higher levels of follower engagement, job satisfaction, and organizational performance. However, the model also recognizes that different situations may require different leadership styles and that effective leaders must be able to adapt their style to fit the needs of their followers and the organization. The Full Range Leadership Model provides a helpful framework for understanding different leadership styles and their impact on organizational outcomes. It emphasizes the importance of building strong relationships with followers, inspiring and motivating them to achieve shared goals, and adapting leadership styles to fit the situation's needs. Situational leadership is separate from situational ethics or a disingenuous approach to leading others. Its focus is optimizing the performance of all the different types of followers by dynamically meeting them where they are.

Let's say you're a military leader, and your job is to take 12 highly trained personnel, including yourself, to the summit of a specific mountain top to set up some critical communications equipment for the ensuing mission. The mountain is very steep, has an elevation of 14,500 feet, and is remote enough that it will require backpacking for 100 miles with everything needed, such as food, water, and shelter for the journey, including the communications equipment to set up at the top.

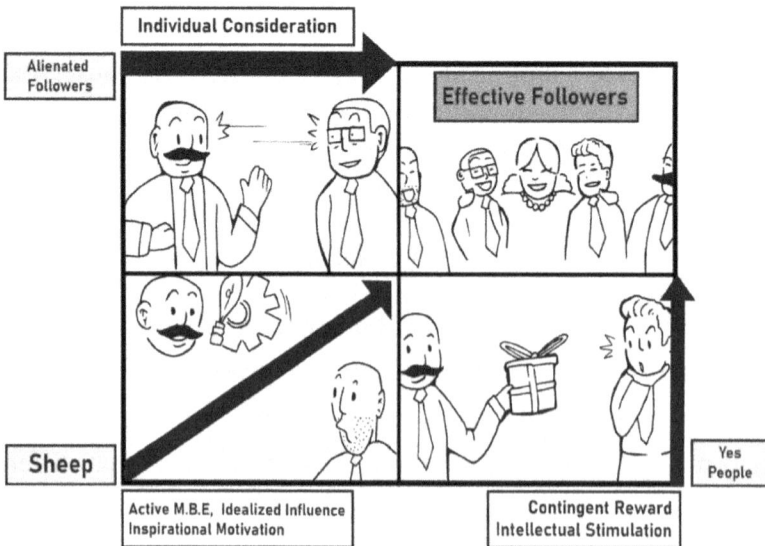

The 11 people following you fall into the Effective follower, Alienated Follower, Sheep, and Yes People categories described in the Dynamic Follower Model.[56] Your goal as a leader is not only to accomplish the mission and set up the communications tower at the top but to help move everyone in the group who is not an "Effective Follower" closer to becoming one. The diagram below encapsulates the different models of leadership and how they would come into play in the communications tower mission.

The next pages show the Lunch Sack Leadership Integrated Leadership Methodology illustration: It combines components of meta-leadership, dynamic followership, and the full-range leadership model. (Pages 108-109)

Intellectual Stimulation (IS): Ask the right technical questions. What are the complexities? Are we climbing the right mountain?

Manage by Exception (MBE-A): Full ruck inspection before we depart. Identify equipment hazard/failure that happen on the trial and repair immediately.

Manage by Exception (MBE-P): No ruck inspection leader waits until team is on trail only to realize some members did not pack enough food and water.

Individual Consideration (IC): How's everyone holding up? I know this is very challenging and strenuous.

Inspirational Motivation (IM): We can do this...can you see how beautiful the view is up here? Look at how well Micah is doing he's making his best time! We will achieve battlefield dominance!

Idealized Influence (II): Lieutenant Rock Climber, twisted his ankle so let's split up his pack load evenly, because we will need his skills at the top to defeat the enemy.

Contingent Reward (CR): When we make it to the top, Susan is buying dinner

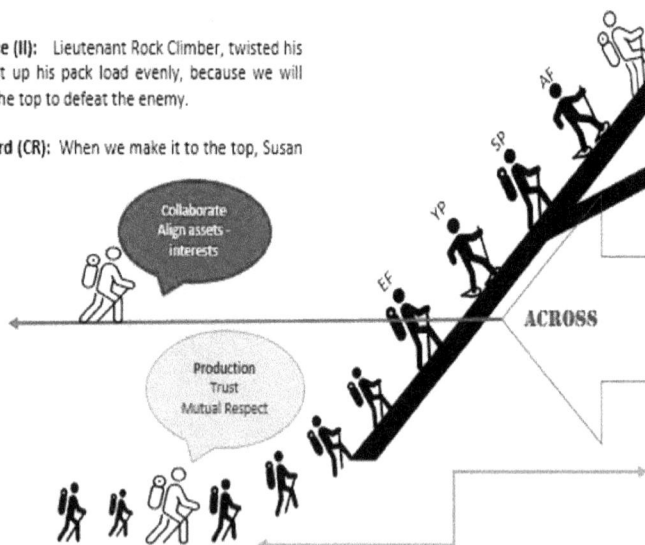

Collaborate
Align assets - interests

Production
Trust
Mutual Respect

ACROSS

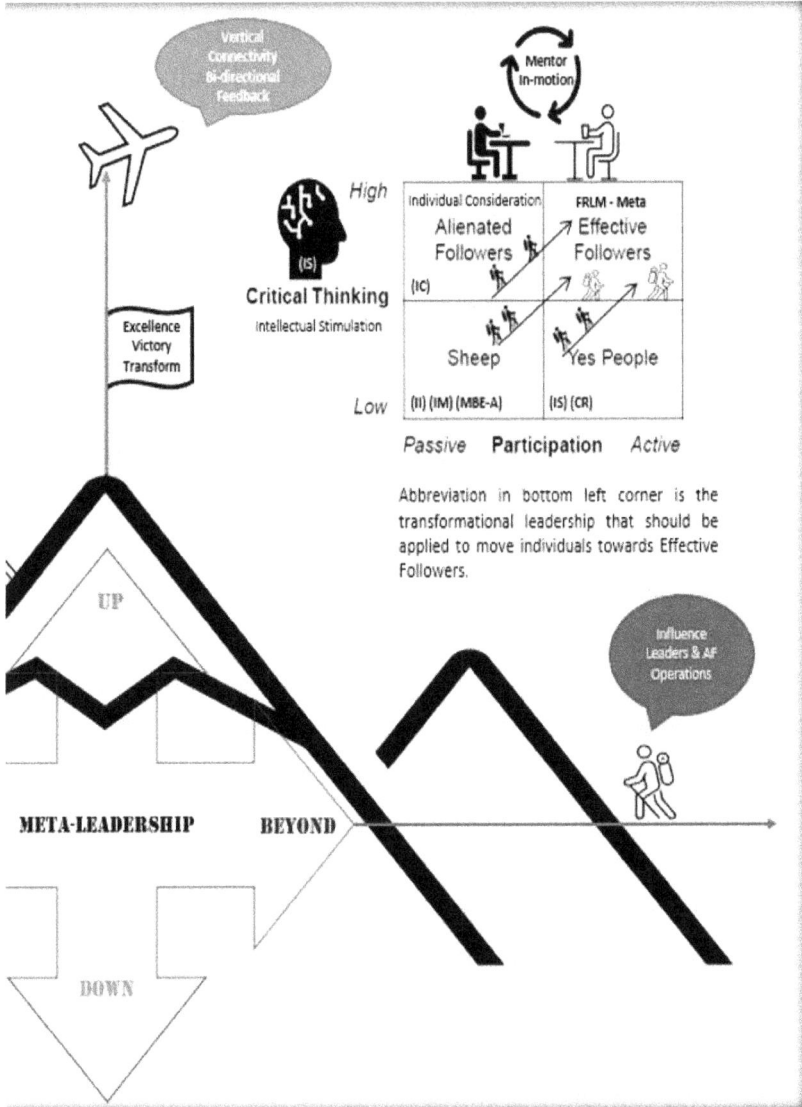

Vertical Connectivity Bi-directional Feedback

Mentor In-motion

High

Critical Thinking
Intellectual Stimulation

Low

(IS)

Excellence Victory Transform

	Individual Consideration	FRLM - Meta
High	Alienated Followers (IC)	Effective Followers
Low	Sheep (II) (IM) (MBE-A)	Yes People (IS) (CR)

Passive **Participation** Active

Abbreviation in bottom left corner is the transformational leadership that should be applied to move individuals towards Effective Followers.

Influence Leaders & AF Operations

UP

META-LEADERSHIP   BEYOND

DOWN

In Chapter 4, we discussed different personality types and used the movie Enter the Dragon with Bruce Lee with the "What's Your Style" video as an example of leadership. While personalities may change slightly over time, the variation within defined personality types is limited. For example, someone who takes the Meyers-Briggs assessment and discovers they're an introvert is unlikely to be assessed later in life as an extrovert. People mature or can remain static over time. If an individual is working on self-awareness and improvement, they will show certain attributes that may not represent their personality type on a continuum. Someone may take an assessment and learn that they're an introvert and very shy and uncomfortable speaking to an audience or giving a presentation. Learning this about themselves and wanting to improve, they enroll in a public speaking class or get involved in a civic organization such as Toastmasters to improve their presentation skills and learn techniques to calm their nerves. They're now outstanding speakers who shine when giving a presentation; they're still introverts when they retake the Meyers-Briggs assessment, but they have matured on the continuum through skill development. Personality types are a part of our genetic makeup and upbringing and generally do not change from the perspective of a scientific psychological assessment. What does change is our ability to grow and mature on a continuum in certain areas. Papa Covey utilized diagram 25 in his 7 Habits book, which is accurate and timeless. Private victories must always precede public victories.

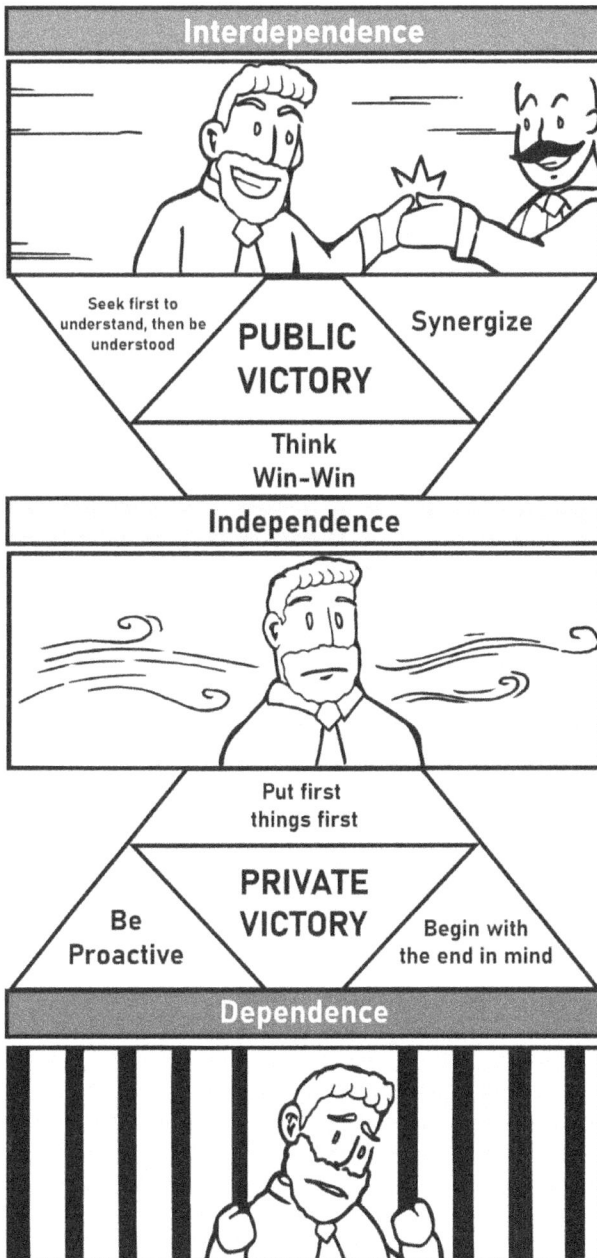

(Adapted from the Seven Habits of Highly Effective People.

-Stephen R. Covey) [57]

Life is a journey, and everyone is at a different time, place, and season in their life. The principles outlined in Lunch Sack Leadership can be applied at any phase of your leadership journey no matter the level of maturity, but there is an underlying assumption that you're functioning above Covey's Independence line as a leader. There is always work to be done in our private lives, but if you're a leader who's deeply struggling to achieve personal, professional, and emotional independence, happiness, and congruity, don't give up. Keep working on yourself and your personal relationships, and you can become the person who finds and fulfills their purpose in life.

Leadership models are different because, unlike personality types, we can choose a preferred method or a combination of several methods or models. The diagram above illustrates this because it encapsulates the use of three different ways that a leader might utilize as one method. Lunch Sack Leadership can be a combination of any of these methods, but there is an emphasis on transformational leadership and a hyper-emphasis on Individual Consideration. Without Individual Consideration, Lunch Sack Leadership is not possible. Individual Consideration is what brings the water to a boil at 212 degrees. The 2-parts hydrogen added to oxygen gives the leadership world water. It provides followers and peers with a peanut butter and jelly sandwich precisely how they prefer it. While all the components of transformational leadership are interdependent, individual consideration asks the leader to adjust their style to fit the individuals they lead best, not just hand everyone the same sandwich.

Everyone who is an alienated follower, sheep, or yes person rather than an effective follower needs you to lead them into the EF zone; applying the same leadership method to each will not get them there. You will thus miss the mark. This requires you to adjust your fire (to use a military term) and utilize Individual Consideration, which could also be described as empathetic listening. The goal is to "seek first to understand" by listening to others. This way, you learn how they prefer to be led and then you adjust your sights and style accordingly. This does not mean lowering your standards or compromising the vision or mission, it means you're taking the time to lead them from the heart. Helping others succeed is who you are, because everyone under your command is going to make it to the top of the mountain. This should be the goal that defines every leader.

CALL TO ACTION:

1. Use the four-quadrant diagram to identify your direct reports or team into the categories of sheep, yes people, alienated followers, and effective followers.
2. Begin developing a preference-based individual consideration plan to move each person into the effective follower's quadrant.

CHAPTER 8

Inversion & Launch

The United States Air Force has its Thunderbirds, and the United States Navy has its Blue Angels. Both are incredible examples of air power and superb aviator skills. The USAF F-15 is a 1980s-era jet that has long been hailed as the most successful dog-fighting aircraft in US history – tallying more than 100 aerial combat victories.

One of the many great scenes in the movie Top Gun is when Maverick and Goose interact with the instructor Charlie and disagree with her about the intelligence information being provided on the MiG. The main character, Pete "Maverick" Mitchell, played by Tom Cruise, discusses the exhilarating experience of flying inverted with his fellow pilots.

The scene takes place during a break from training at the elite Naval Fighter Weapons School, also known as Top Gun. Maverick and his co-pilots are gathered in the briefing room, sharing their stories, and boasting about their flying skills. Maverick, known for his daring and unconventional approach to flying, begins to talk about his encounter with an enemy, MiG, during a previous mission.

He describes how he engaged the enemy aircraft in a dogfight and was disadvantaged. In a daring move, Maverick decides to take the risky maneuver of flying his F-14 Tomcat upside down, or "inverted," to surprise the MiG pilot and gain a tactical advantage so his co-pilot "Goose," could snap a picture of the enemy cockpit. As he describes the moment, the room falls silent, captivated by his audacity, skill and bravado.[58]

The scene not only showcases Maverick's fearless nature and exceptional flying abilities but also reinforces the theme of pushing boundaries and taking risks to become the best fighter pilot. It exemplifies the essence of the movie, which is centered around the intense competition and camaraderie among the Top Gun pilots as they strive for excellence in aerial combat..

The inversion-launch model is based on seven key principles and should be used to design, redesign, or enhance an organization. If you're leading others using preference-based leadership integrated with the inversion-launch model, you will propel your organization, yourself, and others into the stratosphere. Success is measured in parts by wealth and profit, but it's our relationships and spiritual wellness that bring purpose and meaning to life.

1. Servant-Based Command & Control Structure

2. Leadership Development

3. Technical Training

4. Promotion

5. Financial Incentive & Retention Design

6. Communication Structure

7. Recognition

Servant-Based Command & Control Structure

Several works have been published around the concept of an inverted leadership model, which is often depicted as an inverted pyramid. The traditional corporate structure hierarchy has an executive suite, with the CEO and other executives at the top and everyone else reporting up to them in each of their respective disciplines such as finance, marketing, engineering, IT and human resources. Ken Blanchard has written extensively on the subject along with several other authors, such as Robert. K. Greenleaf, Hermann Hesse, Cheryl Bachelder, Liz Wiseman, James Autry, Adam Grant, and many others. This is a movement and system commonly known as Servant Leadership.

The term "servant leadership" was coined by Robert K. Greenleaf, an American author, consultant, and speaker on leadership. In 1970, Greenleaf published an essay called "The Servant as Leader," in which he introduced the concept of servant leadership as a new model of leadership that prioritizes the needs of others before one's own. Greenleaf believed that leaders who embrace the principles of servant leadership would be more effective in creating positive change in organizations and communities and that the world would benefit from more leaders who serve first and lead second. Since Greenleaf introduced the concept, Servant Leadership has become a widely recognized and respected approach to leadership, with many organizations and individuals adopting its principles.

Although Robert Greenleaf coined Servant Leadership, the United States Military has practiced the principles underpinning his original essay and other works since WWII. It's possible that it was used in the military before WWII. Based on my research, experience in the military as an officer and firsthand accounts from retirees and enlisted service people I interviewed; I can trace this style back to World War Two. This is because of my interaction with WWII vets and listening to their stories about how they conducted themselves as leaders.

One might argue that the militaries of any country have the most rigid structure because the entire model is based on rank. The generals are at the top, and everyone else falls in structured rank lines below. It seems counter-intuitive to suggest that an inverted pyramid might exist in the most hierarchal organizations in society. Still, the military is unique in how it indirectly supports this model. They do it without blurring the lines of rank and structure, and it works brilliantly. If you imagine the opposite of the military structure, most people would think of Silicon Valley t-shirt-wearing executives and all wild and unorthodox corporate structures. Do not be afraid because I am happy to introduce you to the Inversion-Launch Model.

The U.S. Military ascension and promotion systems will be used as a primary reference in the Inversion-Launch model, though I'm sure it is relevant for other international militaries. There are several differentiators between corporate and military structures. The first objection one might raise is that if businesses were run like the military, every business would go broke. Be of good cheer, none of the military structures and principles I advocate for will give a venture capitalist or significant corporate shareholder cardiac arrest… quite the opposite. Don't worry if you have never been in the military and don't know anyone who has. The model is for everyone and can be applied, built, and implemented in any organization. The four components of the Inversion-Launch model are Leadership, Ascension, Communication, and Recognition.

Leadership Development – everyone is a leader

One thing that every member of the military has in common is that each branch of service has its own version of an initial indoctrination program, generally referred to as Basic Military

Training (BMT), Boot Camp, Recruit Training, Officer Training School (OTS) or Officer Candidate School (OCS). This training is for a selection of volunteers from all U.S. States and territories, representing every imaginable race, religion, gender, and socioeconomic group. Within the first week of training, the instructors of these courses appoint recruit leaders. Each instructor has approximately 60 recruits in their platoon or flight, which is divided into three to four elements. Each element has an appointed recruit leader, and then a recruit platoon leader is appointed over all the leaders of the elements and given responsibility for all 60 recruits. The number of total recruit leaders for a platoon of 60 would be approximately five, comprising four element leaders and one platoon leader. The recruit platoon leader and any other platoon member take their orders directly from a Military Training Instructor, also known as a Drill Sergeant or Drill Instructor. Recruit leaders are expected to lead. However, without the help of training and drill instructors, there would be chaos because the recruits' knowledge of the military training environment is pretty much zero. Official cleaning duties are also assigned and distributed among the recruits, along with other roles such as guide-on, security guard shifts, chow runner, and dozens of other duties that vary with each service branch. Once a group of recruits occupies their barracks or sleeping quarters, they're 100% responsible for everything that happens inside those walls. Each military branch creates a unique group of tasks and inspectable duties that must be completed every day by the recruits, including taking care of their hygiene. Within each area, there are no less than 100 duties and tasks subject to inspection at any time.

Many may ask why so many minuscule and unimportant details, such as making a bed, cleaning a bathroom, mopping the floor, and shaving, are inspectable, with significant penalties for not doing them correctly. For the U.S Air Force, here's a narrative and an abrasive dialogue between an instructor and recruit that provides an explanation.

A Military Instructor walks into the barracks and inspects the floor to see if it has been properly mopped and polished. 90% of the floor shines so much that the instructor can see their reflection, but then they get to a 10x10 corner section, which has been cleaned by the recruit Lawrence B. Snuffy. It is the primary duty of recruit Johnny A. Merica and several other recruits assigned to ensure the floor is mopped and polished daily. The flight/platoon leader's name is recruit Phil N. Blanks.

Military Instructor (currently standing over the un-polished area in the corner): *"WHERE IS BLANKS? FLIGHT LEADER BLANKS GET OVER HERE NOW!!"*

Recruit Flight Leader Blanks: (walks quickly across barracks and snaps to attention) *"Sir, recruit Blanks reporting as ordered."*

Military Instructor: *"THIS SECTION OF FLOOR LOOKS HORRIBLE – WHY DOES THIS SECTION OF MY FLOOR LOOK SO HORRIBLE?"*

Recruit Flight Leader Blanks: *"Sir, because it was not polished."*

Military Instructor: *"NOOOOOO REALLLLY DO YOU THINK I'M BLIND BLANKS? DO YOU THINK I'M AN IDIOT?"*

Recruit Flight Leader Banks: *"Sir, no, Sir."*

Military Instructor: *"WHO IS RESPONSIBLE FOR POLISHING THE FLOORS BANKS?"*

Recruit Flight Leader Banks: *"Sir, recruit Merica is responsible for polishing the floors."*

Military Instructor: *"RECRUIT MERICA GET OVER HERE NOW!"*

Recruit Merica: (quickly walks across the barracks to the instructor and snaps to attention. Now Blanks and Merica are both at attention over the unpolished area.) *"Sir, recruit Merica reporting as ordered."*

Military Instructor: *"YOU BOTH SUCK!" HOW CAN I TRUST YOU TO WORK ON A 2OO MILLION DOLLAR FIGHTER JET OR A 900 MILLION DOLLAR B-2 WHEN YOU CAN'T EVEN REMEMBER TO PROPERLY SHINE A 10X10 AREA?"*

Now...multiply that by over 100 inspectable items in training, which will provide some context of the expectation. Accountability through inspection. Excellence through inspection. This requires teamwork. Concerning the B-2 Bomber and the F-22 fighter jet, the exact number of items inspected can vary, depending on the type of aircraft and its configuration. The American Federal Aviation Administration typically requires the inspection of thousands of individual items. For example, during a routine maintenance check on a Boeing 737, FAA inspectors may review or test systems such as flight controls, landing gear, engines and auxiliary power units, fuel systems, hydraulic and pneumatic systems, electrical systems, communication and navigation equipment, emergency systems, cabin systems, and components.

The military instructor then administered appropriate punishment to recruits Blanks and Merica, and Snuffy for not being a good team member, mentioning to Merica or Blanks that a section of the floor had been missed. In Basic Military Training, the group of 60 recruits and their peer leaders must learn to delegate and work as a team as quickly as possible. They will learn that succeeding in a military training environment is impossible without working together.

Motivating and leading 60 people who had just met a few days before and who represented every U.S. culture and sub-culture took a lot of work. However, the sooner they learn to work together, the better their chances for achieving excellence. It is universal across the military branches that formal leadership for enlisted personnel begins at about the pay grade of E-4 and is required after every subsequent rank. Leadership is also expected from officers starting at the pay grade of O-1. However, while they may be in-charge of some personnel on paper, O-1's are given little real responsibility until they are mentored and receive some on-the-job training (OJT). It is perfectly normal in the military for formal leadership to be applied within the first four years of service and for it to be done by members who are 25 years old or younger.

Depending on the job and the branch of service, it is common for technically, vocationally trained young, enlisted, and officer personnel from 18-25 years old to be individually responsible for maintaining hundreds of millions of dollars' worth of equipment. Crucially, the stakes are high because if they get it wrong, it could cost people their lives. Quite literally, badly maintained planes can fall out of the sky. Not every job in the military is like this, but there is certainly a fair share of them in every branch, especially the ones who work with nuclear-powered equipment and weapons, such as the Air Force and Navy. This is only possible because of the rigors of training and the established culture from the moment they step off the bus.

A key component of that culture is the expectation of leadership and accountability through inspection. This is very different from the way corporate cultures and structures are formed. Firstly, there is no way that a junior-level employee would be responsible for critical infrastructure and equipment valued at $200+ million. Secondly, there is no expectation that a junior-level employee will be a leader in their first few years of employment. There are some instances of this in retail where a junior associate can be promoted to an assistant manager or manager. Still, it is rare or nonexistent in most corporate structures. In the military, young leaders are mentored and led by older, more experienced leaders both vertically and horizontally by rank, and that lifecycle goes all the way up to the Department Secretaries of every branch, the Secretary of Defense, and all the Chiefs of Staff.

While this hierarchal structure has some rigidity in form, it successfully creates a pipeline filled with the next generation of upcoming leaders, and it's not an insignificant proportion; it's every member of the military that is an E-4 or higher. At the time of writing, there are 1,195,069 members of all U.S. Military branches combined. Leadership development and mentorship are built into the business system of every branch of the military, and it has been this way since its inception. It's leadership by design, and everyone who is an E-4 or higher is being measured against how well they are leading others and helping them reach the next level.

All of this is formally documented in a performance review system. Again, it is like the Sherpa who only keeps track of how many people they've helped climb Mount Everest, not an individual record of their own accomplishments. Individual accomplishments are recorded and counted towards promotion in the military, but the Sherpa example captures the essence of military leadership, which includes mentoring and filling the pipeline with future leaders.

Why would a private company or public-sector agency want to spend that much money and effort on leadership development when most people's tenure at a particular company is only three to five years? They might want to do this because of the time-proven investment technique called "dollar cost averaging." You invest a set amount every week, month, or quarter, regardless of how the market's doing. It is the same for building future leaders. It's why working with HR or Human Capital Management in designing a system that aligns with your business processes by utilizing benchmarking and complexity reduction changes, to name a few, is so important for earnings before interest, taxes, depreciation, and amortization (EBITDA)

A key differentiator with military leadership is that when the leader's followers fail, the leader does not get the luxury of blaming the followers. The leader is fired, not the followers. This is the opposite of what transpires typically in the corporate and public sector where, if the desired or required results still need to be delivered, the leadership at the top makes sweeping cuts and reductions in force. Military leadership demands that accountability be practiced down to the lowest common denominator. This means that, if a troop has minor disciplinary problems, their supervisor is held directly responsible for mentoring and leading them out of the hole, not abandoning them. There is no conference call with human resources where the troop is informed their services are no longer needed. The supervisor sits down with the troop and sets up a performance improvement plan and works to mentor them so they can learn from their mistakes. I can provide dozens of personal examples of this, but here is an account of Larry Mansell, who was promoted to Chief Master Sergeant, which is the highest enlisted rank that can be achieved in the Air Force. This one is particularly meaningful to me because I've served alongside him.

Twenty-one years ago, I was sitting in my chief's office awaiting a decision that could have impacted my career negatively. I had gone on my first Tour of Duty and got into some trouble. I was waiting for my chief to yell at me, call me a screw-up, and kick me out of his unit. I had joined the Air Force about a year earlier with my best friend, JC. We went to basic training together! He helped me realize that this military thing could be a good deal. I wasn't a model airman my first year, but JC ensured I showed up on time (ish) and helped keep me out of trouble (for the most part).

We are all individuals; however, we are all molded by the experiences and people we are around. For example, my mother set my foundation in Faith, my father set my foundation in work ethic (no one will ever out-work him), my grandpa set my foundation in patience, and Chief Ron set my foundation in what a chief is. He told me that day that he would not be kicking me out of his unit; he didn't yell at me. He told me he saw potential in me and wanted to see where I could take that potential. I was blown away that a person of his stature and position would think that about an immature 18-year-old kid. I asked Chief why he would keep me in, and he looked me in my eyes and said, "Because I care about you." Those words have resonated with me ever since. I immediately knew I wanted to be that chief. I wanted to influence people positively, and I have tried to do that throughout all ranks.

So many people in the Aerial Port have shaped/formed me into the NCO I am today.

Cross Training in TACP was bitter-sweet; many officer leaders took a chance on me, and I owe them more than I could ever repay. They have enabled me to join a career field of professionals who have pushed me to be the best version of myself. On 17 March, I reached a milestone I set 21 years ago, as I was leaving my chief's office. I am humbled to join their ranks with all the other chiefs who have mentored me. April 2022 will be 22 years in the Air Force. I can only hope I live up to Chief Ron's expectations!!

-CMSGT. Larry Mansell

Have you been given a second chance or been in the position to give one?

Let's talk about Chief Master Sergeant Ron for a moment. The Chief could have taken the easy route by hammering his troop and coming up with all kinds of justifications for why he "let him go" – and no one would question his reasoning for it. This is the common choice for many managers and leaders who are too lazy to lead. As a co-founder or owner, you may be one of the highest-paid people in your company and consider yourself the brightest. However, if you're not taking the time to lead others truly and you're just giving them lip service, you're a lazy sack of rubbish.

There are leaders who will put less than 5% effort into mentoring their direct reports, and, if they don't show immediate progress, they throw up their hands and come up with all kinds of ridiculous excuses to get rid of them, such as "they were just not a good fit," or "they were under-performing." If this describes you, then you're not a leader. You're a contemptible, smart person with a powerful title. Using your power in this way is the lowest form of leadership, and it makes you a weakling, nothing more than a sometimes-charismatic bean counter who presents well. No one except maybe the board of directors and future romantic partners care about your credentials or where you were educated. Chief Ron was an exemplary leader who took the time to mentor his troop, overcome mistakes, complete one of the most difficult Special Operations training programs in the world, and 21 years later become a Chief himself. This can be your leadership story, too.

127

The Inversion-Launch model design in a corporate structure is based on the servant leadership principles as described by Blanchard, Greenleaf, and others and the well-known inverted pyramid diagram. Still, it includes the traditional vertical triangle pyramid to create a unique parallelogram. The parallelogram represents the dynamic components of business systems and decision-making, some of which retain parts of their hierarchal nature because the market or regulations might demand it. In this model, people are being developed and mentored for leadership in an irreducibly complex process. This process operates constantly, in the same way as a molecular machine like the Kinesin Motor. In his book *Team of Teams,* Stanley McChrystal explores the challenges of leading and operating in complex, fast-moving environments like the battlefield. One of the book's key themes is the importance of combat agility, which McChrystal defines as "the ability to adapt and respond rapidly to changing circumstances."

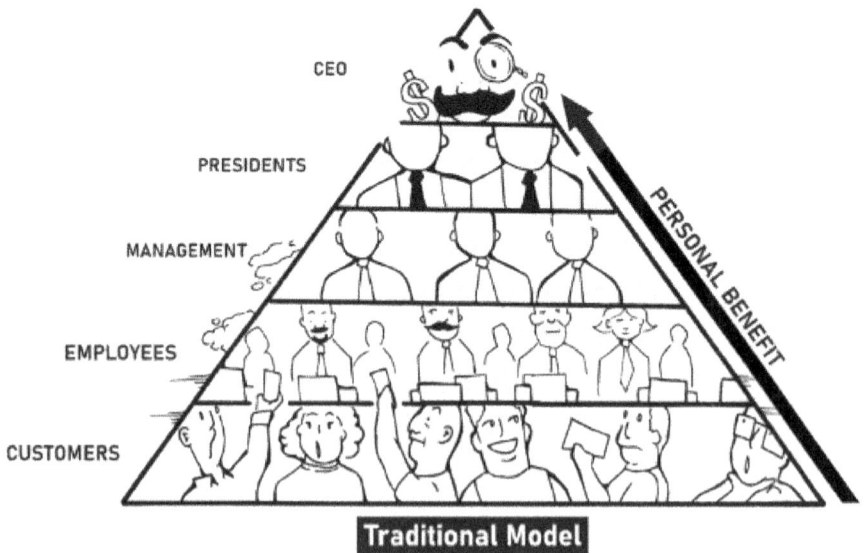

CEO
PRESIDENTS
MANAGEMENT
EMPLOYEES
CUSTOMERS
PERSONAL BENEFIT

Traditional Model

He argues that traditional military structures and processes, which are often hierarchical and bureaucratic, are ill-suited to achieving combat agility in today's fast-paced, unpredictable environments. Instead, he argues for a more networked, decentralized approach to decision-making and problem-solving. In this approach, teams are empowered to make decisions on the ground based on real-time information, and leaders focus on setting clear objectives and providing guidance rather than micromanaging. By decentralizing decision-making and breaking down silos between different teams and departments, organizations can become more agile and responsive to changing circumstances.

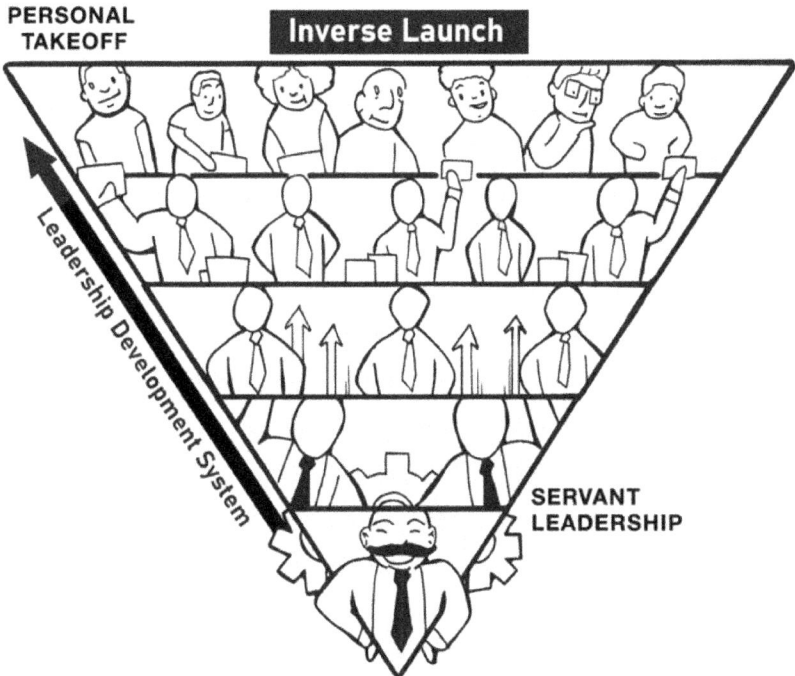

McChrystal also emphasizes the importance of continuous learning and adaptation in achieving combat agility. Rather than relying on rigid plans and procedures, organizations should constantly monitor and adjust their strategies based on new information and feedback. Agility is essential for success in complex environments, and achieving it requires a fundamental shift in organizational culture and leadership approach. It is not just the system that needs to be designed to be agile where possible... what we need is for the leader also to be agile.

The leader in the inversion-launch model must operate in a command-and-control hierarchy when the business system requires it and then traverse the hierarchies downward to empower and develop everyone below. It is the purposeful design of the inversion-launch model that it should mentor and fill the pipeline with future leaders, with an expectation that they will advance. Like the military, this structure is designed intentionally. As future leaders mature in the system, the structure must account for their promotion and "*launching*" to the next level, even if advancement means the person amiably moves-on to another company if an opportunity is not internally available. Steps can be taken to prevent the loss of talented leaders, which I will discuss in the next section.

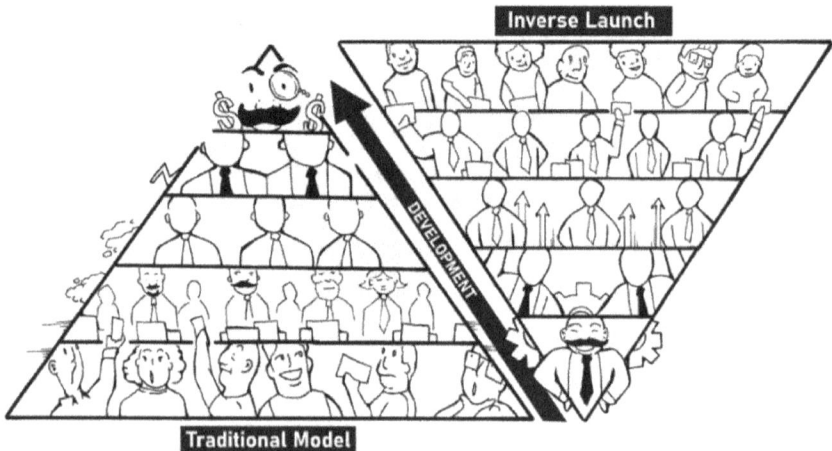

Technical Training & Promotion

One of the things that is almost completely absent in the private sector and in many public sector jobs is a promotion and development structure that resembles the military. What if a new junior-level corporate employee was hired and told that if they showed up to work on time every day and did eight hours of work on a particular set of tasks, they would be guaranteed three raises and promotions in the first four years of employment? How do you think that would impact your EBIDTA and talent retention? This is almost unheard of in corporate and government jobs, but it is precisely what the military does with their new employees. They develop their leadership talent internally from day one. Once an enlisted member or officer signs up and completes their initial vocational and on-the-job training, their first three raises and promotions are guaranteed, barring some disciplinary action. The first four raises and promotions are automatic for many enlisted roles and don't become competitive until E-5. To make E-5 or O-4 in most military branches, you must complete Professional Military Education (PME). Professional Military Education for the U.S. Air Force would consist of the enlisted member attending Airman Leadership School and the officer attending Squadron Officer School. Both schools are instructor-led formal leadership development courses that their peers attend. These courses are not optional; they're full of modern and relevant leadership lessons on team building and interpersonal and personal dynamics. They're a prerequisite to promotion.

For enlisted members, advanced vocational training is also set up in an apprentice, journeyman, craftsman, and superintendent vocational model. These are also prerequisites for advancement. This creates an extremely robust lifecycle of both formal leadership and technical training and, in its basic form, is universal among all military branches. Vocational training includes demonstrated competencies in the knowledge and execution of particular roles. The result is a group of leaders who are all Subject Matter Experts (SMEs). **What are some recent Professional Development courses you have taken?**

LET'S CHAT

The same requirements exist for officers, without some of the vocational components, but branches with warrant officers would be the exception. Before a person can advance to the next rank in the Air Force, they must complete the following leadership development schools. Airman Leadership School (ALS), Non-Commissioned Officer Academy (NCOA), Senior Non-Commissioned Officer Academy (SNCOA) and Chiefs Leadership Course (CLC). For officers, it is Squadron Officer School (SOS), Air Command & Staff College (ACSC), and Air War College (AWC). Bear in mind that someone in the infantry or a combat-related career field will be asked to do some extraordinary things that will not compare to any other corporate or government structure. Every enlisted job in the U.S. Air Force has its own Career Field Education and Training Plan in the same structure with few exceptions.

Just for a moment, imagine a corporate organizational chart where everyone in it has some formal leadership training and all of the managers of people are also Technical Subject Matter Experts in their fields. You know this because your company has paid for their technical certifications and leadership courses and given them the time to attend schools and training. Suppose you're a senior leader in your organization and are doing a re-organization or transformation. What is stopping you from designing a business system that is based on a similar model?

Of course, it would not look exactly like the military, but what if every job in your organization had a purpose-built education and training plan to maximize performance, profit, and happiness? What if your payroll forecasting included employee promotions based on completing pre-defined requirements custom-suited for your business? What if you invested as much in training and leadership as in research and development? The result would be transformational. Our world lacks leaders who have taken the time to do personal and professional development. Toxic and underdeveloped leaders are everywhere, and it makes one wonder how many people currently occupying the C-level executive suites have had any leadership training. Toxic leadership is so pervasive that all kinds of books have been written on the subject. Robert Sutton writes one of the best-known and catchy ones discussed in previous chapters because of the real-life stories it contains. The Stanford Hospital Experiment: One of the key stories in the book is about an experiment at Stanford Hospital, where Dr. Sutton and his colleagues implemented his rule in the workplace. They worked on reducing disruptive and abusive behavior among doctors and nurses, which led to significant improvements in patient care and staff morale.

Despite all the formal training military leaders receive over the years as they ascend through promotions, there are still toxic leaders among the ranks. This is the result of a system failure where rude, dismissive, and condescending behavior is tolerated or where a leader regularly mistreats their colleagues and subordinates and is never confronted: a classic case of conflict avoidance. In the corporate world, an employee would take these types of complaints to their Human Resources Department, whereas, in the military, it would be taken to the Inspector General. The Inspector General acts as a third-party liaison outside the normal change of command to protect people from bias and retribution. The stereotypes of gruff, rude, crass, inconsiderate, and cruel military leaders abound, but like most stereotypes or hasty generalizations, it is mostly untrue. The military no doubt has a unique way of conducting business, but its best leaders are tough because of the high standards for excellence and what's at stake. And they're also kind, considerate, courteous, and mostly friendly. Crucially, they have the courage to make hard decisions.

For the reader who has never been in the military, there are several movies, most of which are based on non-fiction accounts, that I would recommend watching that demonstrate what an excellent, resilient leader looks like in the military. Be aware that some of these movies are quite graphic because war is a gruesome business. Some of the old methods for military discipline are also archaic by any measure.

1. *Saving Private Ryan*
2. *Hacksaw Ridge*
3. *Master & Commander*
4. *The Patriot*
5. *Crimson Tide*
6. *Heartbreak Ridge*
7. *Wind Talkers*
8. *The Band of Brothers Series*
9. *We were Soldiers*
10. *The Great Escape*
11. *Fury*

12. *Glory*
13. *To Hell & Back*
14. *Unbroken*

The list is not exhaustive, and there are many other excellent military leadership movies or books that could probably double or triple the size of the list. Remember, the point of listing these is to provide good examples of both positive and negative leadership. Be mindful that these are made in Hollywood and are played by actors and actresses, so it is essential to be aware that, while they may be based on true stories, they're still movies. You will certainly be entertained by the movies and the excellent acting, but try to watch them with the aim of identifying the leaders and characters and what positive or negative attributes you observe. The movies *The Patriot, Glory*, and Master & Commander are all movies that predate the modern era, so while they both contain excellent examples of military leadership, the current promotion model was not quite the same during the Revolutionary and Civil Wars. They do, however, provide a nice snapshot of military culture and how certain positive leadership qualities have persisted over time in a very old organization.

There are always good and bad guys in military movies because you're always someone's enemy, and the enemies in movies are commonly vilified. For international readers, please bear in mind that several of these American-based military movies are about American colonists and other Americans fighting their fellow countrymen in full-scale war. The emphasis should be on leadership qualities and not the ethnic group or national origin of any particular "enemy" or bad guys portrayed in any movie. Most of the enemies of the past can now be called friends and allies because we have made peace with them.

Financial Incentive & Retention Design

One of the common objections to implementing a robust technical and leadership training program is the argument that if the company pays for advanced technical and leadership training, their employees will get skilled up and leave to work for another organization for better pay. This is seen as a simple supply and demand market equation. This is averted by building a payroll model that factors in the fact that junior-level employees or others joining later in their career are incentivized financially through raises or bonuses for completing the required programs. Another more direct method of retaining employees who receive advanced technical and leadership training is to include a retention system like vesting. For example, if an employee gets certified in several skills and then suddenly leaves, they will have to pay the company back for the cost of the training. If a company invested $25K in training in the employee's first year, a formula would be used to calculate the time required to pay it back. The number might be one to three years, depending on what is fair to the employee and company. This could also be accomplished with a combination of vesting, stock options, partnerships, and succession planning. Again, this would be an excellent way to use a win-win-based strategy to determine what is fair.

Communication – Chain of Command & Empowerment

The best way to lose a battle or fail in business is to communicate poorly. Many who have interacted with military personnel or veterans have come to loathe the use of acronyms. There are so many that they're like the falling green letters and alphanumeric symbols cascading down on the screen in the *Matrix* movies. Every service branch has its own acronyms, and so does every career field. Most would have better luck dumping five cans of SpaghettiOs into a bowl. As frustrating as it can be for someone who is listening from the outside, there is a reason for it: it functions as a form of shorthand.

The military's command-and-control structure in combat requires communication to occur in the quickest, most concise manner possible. This is where seconds matter, and accuracy is paramount because of the stakes. Like a court reporter using shorthand, the use of shortened communication methods has pervaded every branch of military culture because of its necessity in combat. It is so embedded that it is continually used by everyone, even when not in combat.

Acronyms are everywhere, from supply to finance to all other administrative duties. It can be quite entertaining listening to military people talk and rattle off a bunch of phrases and sentences that make absolutely no sense to anyone. Don't be fooled because if they're from different service branches, they might be nodding their heads in agreement but still have no idea what the other branches' acronyms mean either. You can imagine how difficult this would be in combat when working with another service branch, which is another thing Stanley McChrystal addresses in his *Team of Teams*. This is why the military has developed extensive training around joint operations communication methods. History is full of military battles lost unnecessarily because of poor communication. One of the more famous ones is the Charge of the Light Brigade. This was a military engagement that took place on October 25, 1854, during the Crimean War. The charge was an ill-fated attempt by British cavalry to attack Russian artillery positions during the Battle of Balaclava.

The charge was ordered by British commander Lord Raglan, who intended for the Light Brigade to advance down a different route and attack the Russian positions at the end. However, due to a miscommunication, the order failed to be understood, and the Light Brigade instead charged directly at the Russian guns. This was a disastrous mistake, as the cavalry was outnumbered and outgunned by the Russian artillery. The Light Brigade suffered heavy casualties, with more than 100 men killed and over 150 wounded. The charge became famous for its bravery in the face of overwhelming odds, as the British soldiers charged towards certain death. It is remembered as a tragic mistake that resulted in unnecessary loss of life. The event highlighted the need for clear communication and planning in military operations, and it served as a cautionary tale for future military engagements.

In business, concise communication is just as important as in the digital age. It has become increasingly challenging because of information saturation. In short, the worker is overstimulated by dozens of forms of media. What is the formula for creating lean communication? Lean methodology is a business strategy and management approach that emphasizes the continuous improvement of processes and eliminating waste to maximize customer efficiency and value. The goal is to create a culture of continuous improvement that focuses on delivering high-quality products or services to customers while minimizing waste and reducing costs. The origins of lean methodology can be traced back to the Toyota Production System, which Japanese engineer Taiichi Ohno developed in the 1940s. The system emphasized the importance of continuous improvement and waste reduction in manufacturing processes. Lean methodology is characterized by five key principles, two of which are Value Stream and Flow. Value Stream involves mapping the value and identifying areas of waste, inefficiency, and bottlenecks in order to streamline processes and eliminate waste. Flow creates a smooth and continuous flow of work by eliminating interruptions, delays, and obstacles.

The military uses highly structured communication methods that allow information to flow up and down the chain of command. There are plenty of areas where the military does this excellently and others where the structure itself is the problem. One of the key differentiators in military communication is how everyone is trained to follow the chain of command in daily operations. This chain of command system may only increase the time taken to communicate with someone when speed is preferred. Still, it is a model that uses a lowest-common-denominator framework, which is quite effective. For example, it is required that a military member talk first to their direct supervisor if they have a question or problem, and they would usually have the answer. If not, the supervisor would escalate, if necessary, talk to the next level, and keep escalating until there's an answer. Strict discipline is applied if you do not speak to the direct supervisor and instead go two or three levels above them with an issue. It is a sure-fire way to be reprimanded.

All members enforce this structure so well that when they approach the leaders who are higher ranking, the first thing they will ask is, "Have you talked to your supervisor?" If the answer to that question is no, buckle up for negative consequences. Of course, there are always exceptions to the rule, but respect for the order of chain-of-command communication is universal. Empowering people throughout the chain of command requires a mature, non-toxic leader who has created psychological safety and a culture of respect, dignity, and excellence.

In business and other environments in the public and private sector, if employees constantly have to escalate issues, it's because their direct supervisor hasn't been trained or properly empowered to make decisions. You will find this to be pervasive in companies with toxic leadership and cultures of fear where people cower when asked to make a business decision. This is because they're afraid for their jobs, or they're always copying leadership in communication for CYA. Analyzing how many tasks require next-level approval would be a quick and easy method for capturing the morale and pulse of an organization.

The most effective military organizations across the branches are the ones that empower personnel to the lowest common denominator to make decisions. This is true among all of America's most elite forces that belong to the United States Special Operations Command, responsible for coordinating and conducting special operations and unconventional warfare. It is comprised of several component commands, which include Army Special Operations Command (Green Berets & Airborne Rangers), Naval Special Warfare Command (SEALS), Air Force Special Operations Command (Combat Control, Pararescue, JTAC, AC-

130), Marine Corps Forces Special Operations Command (RECON) and Joint Special Operations Command. Remember, this delegated decision-making and communication is a result of an investment in leadership and technical training along with high levels of demonstrated competency.

Turn the Ship Around! is a book by David Marquet, a former submarine commander in the United States Navy. He discusses his experience turning around the culture and performance of the USS Santa Fe. This submarine was initially plagued by low morale, poor performance, and a high rate of turnover. Marquet implemented a leadership model that shifted the focus from a top-down, hierarchical approach to a more decentralized, empowering one. He gave his crew members more autonomy and responsibility, encouraging them to take ownership of their roles and make decisions on their own. He also strongly emphasized training and developing his crew, providing them with the tools and resources they needed to succeed. Through this approach, Marquet was able to create a culture of excellence. The submarine achieved the highest retention rate in the Navy, won multiple awards for its performance, and was recognized as one of the most effective submarines in the fleet.

Recognition

It should come as no surprise that members of the United States Military are not paid the same as those who work in the private sector and many other public sector jobs. It long proves the point about the impact of competitive recruiting and hiring talented and skilled individuals that it is only sometimes about the compensation package. This is why it is called serving your country and not working for it. So how can an organization pay people less and still retain them for 20 or 30 years? Firstly, as discussed previously, they're provided with a clear path for advancement, so their pay should not stay static for more than four years. As mentioned, they will initially receive two to three raises within four years. As they achieve higher ranks, they compete with their peers and are promoted based on achievement and completing professional military education and advanced technical vocational training. An entire promotion structure for this is routinely analyzed for fairness and occasionally adjusted as needed. Secondly, if an individual is performing well, they're recognized by a very formal process called awards and decorations. There are quarterly and yearly awards for every rank, and it is divided as follows: junior enlisted, non-commissioned officer, senior non-commissioned officer, company grade officer, and field grade officers. The four quarterly award winners' packages are rated, the candidates are interviewed and scored, and a board selects a yearly award winner for each rank.

Based on the numbers above, there would be 20 quarterly award winners for each year, and five would be selected as the yearly award winner. These annual award winners then compete nationally, where they can be selected as the winner of the same award for a Major Command and then again for a national award, all competing against peers.

Depending on the size of your company or public sector organization, a recognition program of this scale might be difficult. It could create competition that would result in negative cultural outcomes if incorrectly designed. Each business or organization would need to design something that best suited their needs but still carried weight and some measure of difficulty in attaining the award. If it's too easy to win the recognition, it diminishes the value.

Another way that the military recognizes individuals and teams is by presenting them with medals that they display on their dress uniforms. The history of the United States Armed Forces medal system dates back to the Revolutionary War when soldiers were awarded badges of distinction for their service. Over time, the medal system evolved to include a wide range of awards and decorations, each with its own criteria for eligibility and design. One of the earliest medals established was the Purple Heart, first introduced by General George Washington in 1782 to recognize soldiers who had been wounded or killed in action. In 1932, the award was expanded to include military personnel killed or wounded due to hostile action. The United States Armed Forces medal system includes a wide range of other awards and decorations, such as the Silver Star, the Bronze Star, and the Distinguished Service Cross. These medals are awarded for various acts of valor, meritorious service, and achievements in specific areas. The criteria for eligibility and design of these medals have been updated and revised over time to reflect changes in military operations and technology. Today, the United States Armed Forces medal system remains an important way of recognizing and honoring the sacrifices and achievements of military personnel.

Does your company or business have a recognition program? One of the best recognition programs I've experienced in the corporate sector was when I was a leader at Hitachi Vantara. If an employee was performing exceptionally, I had the discretion to send them a thank you with a $150-200 gift card for dinner at any time. At the end of the year, I was encouraged to distribute financial awards to excellent employees with gifts in the range of $1,500, $2,500, and $5,000. They would provide me with a limited number of these awards and would tell me to distribute them to whoever I thought best deserved them. This was in addition to their normal structured quarterly bonuses. Dozens of companies regularly do the same, many of which are in the Fortune 500 or 100. A robust recognition program is one of the key elements of the Inversion-Launch model because it is important for retention and creates a system where high performance becomes part of the culture.

Becoming a more effective leader is challenging but will enable personal and organizational transformation over time. This book encompasses valuable insights, including exercises on self-awareness, the six principles of hospitality, contrasted with the five traditional "old school" leadership attributes, and an examination of the seven aspects of toxic leadership. Additionally, the book delves into the five elements of Dynamic followership, offering a detailed exploration of various follower types and effective leadership approaches for each.

The inversion-launch approach is built upon seven fundamental principles. These principles can be effectively employed when crafting, reorganizing, or enhancing a company or organization. By integrating preference-based leadership with the inversion-launch methodology, one can propel the organization and oneself to unprecedented heights.

CALL TO ACTION: Perform an analysis of your entire Org Structure and Business Systems. Explore where the Inversion-Launch Method can be implemented.

LET'S CHAT

Appendix:

Suggested Books on Spirituality

God's Universe *by Owen Gingerich*

Sacred Pathways *by Gary Thomas*

Everyday Holiness: The Jewish Spiritual Path of Mussar

by Alan Morinis, Jonathan Davis, et al.

END NOTES

[1] 15 Different Types of Bread - Katom Learning Center. Accessed February 8, 2023. https://www.katom.com/learning-center/15-different-types-of-bread.html. 8: 37 PM CST

[2] High Protein Peanut Butter – All You Need to Know. Alpino Foods. Accessed February 8, 2023. https://alpino.store/blogs/news/high-protein-peanut-butter-all-you-need-to-know#:~:text=The%20grocery%20store%20shelves%20are,and%20even%20p owdered%20peanut%20butter. 8:53 PM CST.

[3] 57 Jams, Jellies & Fruity Spreads to Make this Spring. Accessed February 8, 2023. https://www.tasteofhome.com/collection/spring-jams-jellies-fruity-spreads 9:07 PM CST

[4] Amendt, Linda J. 175 Best Jams, Jellies, Marmalades & Other Soft Spreads. Toronto: R. Rose, 2008.

[5] Sinek, Simon. Leaders Eat Last: Why Some Teams Pull Together and Others Don't. London: Penguin Business, 2019.

[6] Bible Gateway Passage: Ecclesiastes 5:12 - New King James Version." Bible Gateway. Accessed February 11, 2023. https://www.biblegateway.com/passage/?search=Ecclesiastes+5%3A12&vers ion=NKJV. 10:37 AM CST

[7] Yohn, Denise L. "Company Culture Is Everyone's Responsibility; A top-down approach doesn't work anymore." Accessed February 11, 2023, https://hbsp.harvard.edu/product/H065SN-PDF-ENG Feb 8, 2021. 10:52 AM CST.

[8] The 16 Types of Meetings. Accessed February 11, 2023. https://www.lucidmeetings.com/meeting-types. 11:23 AM CST

[9] The 16 Types of Meetings. Accessed February 11, 2023. https://blog.lucidmeetings.com/blog/16-types-of-business meetings/#:~:text=Every%20type%20of%20meeting%20has,encourag ed%2C%20gets%20the%20best%20results. 11:27 AM CST

[10] The 16 Types of Meetings. Accessed February 11, 2023
https://blog.lucidmeetings.com/blog/16-types-of-business
meetings/#:~:text=Every%20type%20of%20meeting%20has,encouraged%2C%20gets%20the%20best%20results. 11:31 AM CST

[11] Covey, Stephen R. The 7 Habits of Highly Effective People. London: Simon & Schuster UK Ltd., 2020. Pages 222, 218, 219, 220. Kindle

[12] Covey, Stephen R. The 7 Habits of Highly Effective People. London: Simon & Schuster UK Ltd., 2020. Pages 222, 218, 219, 220. Kindle

[13] Covey, Stephen R. The 7 Habits of Highly Effective People. London: Simon & Schuster UK Ltd., 2020. Pages 222, 218, 219, 220. Kindle

[14] Dalio, Ray. Principles Life and Work. Malmö: MTM, 2020.

[15] "Dr. Deming's 14 Points for Management." The W. Edwards Deming Institute. Accessed February 12, 2023. https://deming.org/explore/fourteen-points/. 1:47 PM CST

[16] Covey, Stephen R. The 7 Habits of Highly Effective People. London: Simon & Schuster UK Ltd., 2020. Page 220. Kindle

[17] Covey, Stephen R. The 7 Habits of Highly Effective People. London: Simon & Schuster UK Ltd., 2020. Page 220. Kindle

[18] Enter the Dragon, Directed by Robert Clouse, performance by Bruce Lee & Peter Archer Warner Bros/Concord Productions/Sequoia Pictures. 1973.

[19] Simon Sinek, "Leaders Eat Last; Why Some Teams Pull Together and Others Don't" Penguin Group Publishing 2014.

[20] Tuckman, Bruce (1965). "Developmental sequence in small groups". Psychological Bulletin. 63 (6): 384–399. doi:10.1037/h0022100. PMID 14314073. Reprinted with permission in Group Facilitation, Spring 2001

[21] O. P., John, &, S. Srivastava, The Big-Five trait taxonomy: History, measurement, and
theoretical perspectives. In L. A. Pervin & O. P. John (Eds.), Handbook of personality: Theory
and research (Vol. 2, pp. 102–138). (1999). New York: Guilford Press.

[22] "The HEXACO Personality Inventory - Revised." The HEXACO Personality Inventory - Revised. Accessed February 25, 2023. https://hexaco.org/hexaco-online. 9:32 AM CST

[23] "Hogan Personality Inventory." Hogan Assessments. Accessed February 25, 2023. https://www.hoganassessments.com/assessment/hogan-personality-inventory/.   9:37 AM CST

[24] Myers & Briggs Foundation. "Myers-Briggs® Overview." Myers Briggs Type Preferences Perception Judgment. Myers & Briggs Foundation, n.d. Accessed February 25, 2023. https://www.myersbriggs.org/my-mbti-personality-type/myers-briggs-overview/. 9:39 AM CST

[25] "What Is the Disc Assessment?" Discprofile.Com. Accessed February 25, 2023. https://www.discprofile.com/what-is-disc. 10:33 AM CST.

[26] "How to Communicate Effectively with Everyone You Lead." 5 Voices. Accessed February 25, 2023. https://5voices.com/. 11:09 AM CST

[27] Sutton, Robert I., The No Asshole Rule: Building a Civilized Workplace and Surviving One That Isn't. Business Plus; 1st edition (February 22, 2007). Page 49, Kindle.

[28] Sutton, Robert I., The No Asshole Rule: Building a Civilized Workplace and Surviving One That Isn't. Business Plus; 1st edition (February 22, 2007). Page 49, Kindle.

[29] Duckworth, Angela. Grit: Why Passion and Resilience Are the Secrets to Success. London: Vermilion, 2017.

[30] Anderson, Chris, The Long Tail: Why the Future of Business Is Selling Less of More. Hyperion 2006.

[31] "The Long Tail Theory, Debunked: We Stick With What We Know." Accessed March 5, 2023. https://mackinstitute.wharton.upenn.edu/2018/long-tail-theory/ 5:57 PM CST

[32] "Japan's Secret: W Edwards Deming," Accessed March 5, 2023 https://www.washingtonpost.com/archive/opinions/1993/12/23/japans-secret-w-edwards-deming/b69b8c00-4c5d-483a-b95e-4aeb1d94d2c6/ 6:32 PM CST

[33] "Japan's Secret: W Edwards Deming," Accessed March 5, 2023 https://www.washingtonpost.com/archive/opinions/1993/12/23/japans-secret-w-edwards-deming/b69b8c00-4c5d-483a-b95e-4aeb1d94d2c6/ 6:32 PM CST

[34] Duckworth, Angela. Grit: The Power of Passion and Perseverance (pp. 30-31). Scribner. Kindle Edition.

[35] Sutton, Robert I., The No Asshole Rule: Building a Civilized Workplace and Surviving One That Isn't. Business Plus; 1st edition (February 22, 2007).

[36] Kubicek, Jeremie, The 100X Leader: How to Become Someone Worth Following. Wiley; 1st edition (March 26, 2019) Audible Edition.

[37] "Multi-Source assessment and Feedback." Accessed March 10, 2023 https://www.rand.org/content/dam/rand/pubs/research_reports/RR900/RR998/RAND_RR998.pdf 9:35 PM CST.

[38] "Defense Organizational Climate Survey. " Accessed March 10, 2023. https://www.opa.mil/research-analysis/opa-surveys/defense-organizational-climate-survey 9:53 PM CST.

[39] "Behavioral Event Interview." Accessed March 11, 2023. https://toolkit.vets.syr.edu/wp-content/uploads/2012/11/Tool-BEI-Toolkit.pdf 10:07 AM CST.

[40] Leader 360 Assessment." Accessed March 11, 2023. https://www.qualtrics.com/experience-management/employee/360-reviews-leadership/ 10:37 AM CST

[41] "Organizational Culture Assessment Instrument." Accessed March 11, 2023 https://www.ocai-online.com/about-the-Organizational-Culture-Assessment-Instrument-OCAI 10:51 AM CST

[42] McKee, Annie, "Quiz Yourself: Do You Lead with Emotional Intelligence?" https://hbr.org/2015/06/quiz-yourself-do-you-lead-with-emotional-intelligence 11:03 AM CST

[43] Leadership Effectiveness Analysis:" Accessed March 11, 2023 https://www.mrg.com/assessments/leadership/ 1:31 PM CST.

[44] Ray Dalio, "Principles: Life and Work." Simon & Shuster, September 19, 2017

[45] James Clear "Atomic Habits: An Easy & Proven Way to Build Good Habits & Break Bad Ones" Avery; First Edition (October 16, 2018)

[46] Stanley McChrystal, " Team of Teams: New Rules of Engagement for a Complex World." Portfolio; Illustrated edition (May 12, 2015)

[47] Marcus, Leonard J.; Dorn, Barry C.; Henderson, Joseph M. (2006-06-01). "Meta-Leadership and National Emergency Preparedness: A Model to Build Government Connectivity". Biosecurity and Bioterrorism: Biodefense Strategy, Practice, and Science. 4 (2): 128–134. CiteSeerX 10.1.1.558.6326. doi:10.1089/bsp.2006.4.128. ISSN 1538-7135. PMID 16792480.

[48] Latour, Sharon, M. Lt. Col, USAF; Rast J. Vicky Lt. Col. USAF. Dynamic Followership, The Prerequisite for Effective Leadership. Air & Space Power Journal. (Winter 2004).

[49] Kelley, Robert E. "In Praise of Followers," in Military Leadership: In Pursuit of Excellence, 3rd ed., ed. Robert L. Taylor and William E. Rosenbach (Boulder, CO: Westview Press, 1996), 136–37.

[50] Kelley, Robert E. "In Praise of Followers," in Military Leadership: In Pursuit of Excellence, 3rd ed., ed. Robert L. Taylor and William E. Rosenbach (Boulder, CO: Westview Press, 1996), 136–37.

[51] Kelley, Robert E. "In Praise of Followers," in Military Leadership: In Pursuit of Excellence, 3rd ed., ed. Robert L. Taylor and William E. Rosenbach (Boulder, CO: Westview Press, 1996), 136–37.

[52] Developing Your Full Range of Leadership: Leveraging a Transformational Approach Dr. Fil J. Arenas, Lt Col Daniel Connelly, USAF and Maj Michael D. Williams, USAF, August 2014. Pg 9, 13, 14, 18.

[53] Developing Your Full Range of Leadership: Leveraging a Transformational Approach Dr. Fil J. Arenas, Lt Col Daniel Connelly, USAF and Maj Michael D. Williams, USAF, August 2014. Pg 9, 13, 14, 18.

[54] Developing Your Full Range of Leadership: Leveraging a Transformational Approach Dr. Fil J. Arenas, Lt Col Daniel Connelly, USAF and Maj Michael D. Williams, USAF, August 2014. Pg 9, 13, 14, 18.

[55] Developing Your Full Range of Leadership: Leveraging a Transformational Approach Dr. Fil J. Arenas, Lt Col Daniel Connelly, USAF and Maj Michael D. Williams, USAF, August 2014. Pg 9, 13, 14, 18.

[56] Latour, Sharon, M. Lt. Col, USAF; Rast J. Vicky Lt. Col. USAF. Dynamic Followership, The Prerequisite for Effective Leadership. Air & Space Power Journal. (Winter 2004).

[57] Covey, Stephen R. The 7 Habits of Highly Effective People. London: Simon & Schuster UK Ltd., 2020. Diagram 25.

.

www.ingramcontent.com/pod-product-compliance
Lightning Source LLC
Chambersburg PA
CBHW070043100426
42740CB00013B/2781